M000318136

The Poems of Emma Lazarus

VOLUME II

Jewish Poems and Translations

DOVER · THRIFT · EDITIONS

The Poems of Emma Lazarus

VOLUME II

Jewish Poems and Translations

DOVER PUBLICATIONS, INC.
Mineola, New York

DOVER THRIFT EDITIONS

GENERAL EDITOR: MARY CAROLYN WALDREP
EDITOR OF THIS VOLUME: SUSAN L. RATTINER

Copyright

Copyright © 2015 by Dover Publications, Inc.
All rights reserved.

Bibliographical Note

This Dover edition, first published in 2015, is an unabridged republication of the work originally published by Houghton Mifflin Company, Boston and New York, in 1889.

Library of Congress Cataloging-in-Publication Data

Lazarus, Emma, 1849–1887.
    [Poems. Selections]
    The Poems of Emma Lazarus. Volume II, Jewish Poems and Translations / Emma Lazarus.
        pages cm. — (Dover Thrift Editions)
    ISBN-13: 978-0-486-78643-8 (paperback)
    ISBN-10: 0-486-78643-9 (paperback)
    I. Rattiner, Susan L., editor. II. Title.

PS2233.A4 2015
811'.4—dc23

                                                                        2014024337

Manufactured in the United States by Courier Corporation
78643901   2015
www.doverpublications.com

CONTENTS.

———◆———

Most of the poems in this volume were originally printed in "The American Hebrew."

THE NEW YEAR.

ROSH—HASHANAH, 5643.

NOT while the snow-shroud round dead earth is
    rolled,
  And naked branches point to frozen skies, —
When orchards burn their lamps of fiery gold,
  The grape glows like a jewel, and the corn
A sea of beauty and abundance lies,
        Then the new year is born.

Look where the mother of the months uplifts
  In the green clearness of the unsunned West,
Her ivory horn of plenty, dropping gifts,
  Cool, harvest-feeding dews, fine-winnowed
    light;
Tired labor with fruition, joy and rest
        Profusely to requite.

Blow, Israel, the sacred cornet! Call
  Back to thy courts whatever faint heart throb
With thine ancestral blood, thy need craves all.
  The red, dark year is dead, the year just born
Leads on from anguish wrought by priest and
    mob,
        To what undreamed-of morn?

For never yet, since on the holy height,
   The Temple's marble walls of white and green
Carved like the sea-waves, fell, and the world's
     light
   Went out in darkness, — never was the year
Greater with portent and with promise seen,
       Than this eve now and here.

Even as the Prophet promised, so your tent
   Hath been enlarged unto earth's farthest rim.
To snow-capped Sierras from vast steppes ye
     went,
   Through fire and blood and tempest-tossing
     wave,
For freedom to proclaim and worship Him,
      Mighty to slay and save.

High above flood and fire ye held the scroll,
   Out of the depths ye published still the Word.
No bodily pang had power to swerve your soul :
   Ye, in a cynic age of crumbling faiths,
Lived to bear witness to the living Lord,
      Or died a thousand deaths.

In two divided streams the exiles part,
   One rolling homeward to its ancient source,
One rushing sunward with fresh will, new heart.
   By each the truth is spread, the law unfurled,
Each separate soul contains the nation's force,
      And both embrace the world.

Kindle the silver candle's seven rays,
　Offer the first fruits of the clustered bowers,
The garnered spoil of bees. With prayer and
　　　praise
　Rejoice that once more tried, once more we
　　　prove
How strength of supreme suffering still is ours
　　　For Truth and Law and Love.

THE CROWING OF THE RED COCK.

Across the Eastern sky has glowed
　The flicker of a blood-red dawn,
Once more the clarion cock has crowed,
　Once more the sword of Christ is drawn.
A million burning rooftrees light
The world-wide path of Israel's flight.

Where is the Hebrew's fatherland?
　The folk of Christ is sore bestead;
The Son of Man is bruised and banned,
　Nor finds whereon to lay his head.
His cup is gall, his meat is tears,
His passion lasts a thousand years.

Each crime that wakes in man the beast,
　Is visited upon his kind.
The lust of mobs, the greed of priest,
　The tyranny of kings, combined

To root his seed from earth again,
His record is one cry of pain.

When the long roll of Christian guilt
　　Against his sires and kin is known,
The flood of tears, the life-blood spilt,
　　The agony of ages shown,
What oceans can the stain remove,
From Christian law and Christian love?

Nay, close the book; not now, not here,
　　The hideous tale of sin narrate,
Reëchoing in the martyr's ear,
　　Even he might nurse revengeful hate,
Even he might turn in wrath sublime,
With blood for blood and crime for crime.

Coward?　Not he, who faces death,
　　Who singly against worlds has fought,
For what?　A name he may not breathe,
　　For liberty of prayer and thought.
The angry sword he will not whet,
His nobler task is — to forget.

IN EXILE.

"Since that day till now our life is one unbroken paradise. We live a true brotherly life. Every evening after supper we take a seat under the mighty oak and sing our songs. — *Extract from a letter of a Russian refugee in Texas.*

TWILIGHT is here, soft breezes bow the grass,
    Day's sounds of various toil break slowly off,
The yoke-freed oxen low, the patient ass
    Dips his dry nostril in the cool, deep trough.
Up from the prairie the tanned herdsmen pass
    With frothy pails, guiding with voices rough
Their udder-lightened kine. Fresh smells of
        earth,
The rich, black furrows of the glebe send forth.

After the Southern day of heavy toil,
    How good to lie, with limbs relaxed, brows
        bare
To evening's fan, and watch the smoke-wreaths
        coil
    Up from one's pipe-stem through the rayless air.
So deem these unused tillers of the soil,
    Who stretched beneath the shadowing oak-
        tree, stare
Peacefully on the star-unfolding skies,
And name their life unbroken paradise.

The hounded stag that has escaped the pack,
    And pants at ease within a thick-leaved dell;

The unimprisoned bird that finds the track
   Through sun-bathed space, to where his fellows
      dwell ;
The martyr, granted respite from the rack,
   The death-doomed victim pardoned from his
      cell, —
Such only know the joy these exiles gain, —
Life's sharpest rapture is surcease of pain.

Strange faces theirs, wherethrough the Orient
      sun
   Gleams from the eyes and glows athwart the
    skin.
Grave lines of studious thought and purpose
      run
   From curl-crowned forehead to dark-bearded
    chin.
And over all the seal is stamped thereon
   Of anguish branded by a world of sin,
In fire and blood through ages on their name,
Their seal of glory and the Gentiles' shame.

Freedom to love the law that Moses brought,
   To sing the songs of David, and to think
The thoughts Gabirol to Spinoza taught,
   Freedom to dig the common earth, to drink
The universal air — for this they sought
   Refuge o'er wave and continent, to link
Egypt with Texas in their mystic chain,
And truth's perpetual lamp forbid to wane.

Hark! through the quiet evening air, their song
　　Floats forth with wild sweet rhythm and glad
　　　　refrain.
They sing the conquest of the spirit strong,
　　The soul that wrests the victory from pain;
The noble joys of manhood that belong
　　To comrades and to brothers. In their strain
Rustle of palms and Eastern streams one hears,
And the broad prairie melts in mist of tears.

IN MEMORIAM — REV. J. J. LYONS.

ROSH-HASHANAH, 5638.

THE golden harvest-tide is here, the corn
Bows its proud tops beneath the reaper's hand.
Ripe orchards' plenteous yields enrich the land;
Bring the first fruits and offer them this morn,
With the stored sweetness of all summer hours,
The amber honey sucked from myriad flowers,
And sacrifice your best first fruits to-day,
With fainting hearts and hands forespent with
　　toil,
Offer the mellow harvest's splendid spoil,
To Him who gives and Him who takes away.

Bring timbrels, bring the harp of sweet accord,
And in a pleasant psalm your voice attune,
And blow the cornet greeting the new moon.
Sing, holy, holy, holy, is the Lord,
Who killeth and who quickeneth again,

Who woundeth, and who healeth mortal pain,
Whose hand afflicts us, and who sends us peace.
Hail thou slim arc of promise in the West,
Thou pledge of certain plenty, peace, and rest.
With the spent year, may the year's sorrows
      cease.

For there is mourning now in Israel,
The crown, the garland of the branching tree
Is plucked and withered.   Ripe of years was he.
The priest, the good old man who wrought so
      well
Upon his chosen glebe.   For he was one
Who at his seed-plot toiled through rain and
      sun.
Morn found him not as one who slumbereth,
Noon saw him faithful, and the restful night
Stole o'er him at his labors to requite
The just man's service with the just man's death.

What shall be said when such as he do pass ?
Go to the hill-side, neath the cypress-trees,
Fall midst that peopled silence on your knees,
And weep that man must wither as the grass.
But mourn him not, whose blameless life com-
      plete
Rounded its perfect orb, whose sleep is sweet,
Whom we must follow, but may not recall.
Salute with solemn trumpets the New Year,
And offer honeyed fruits as were he here,
Though ye be sick with wormwood and with gall.

THE VALLEY OF BACA.

PSALM LXXXIV.

A BRACKISH lake is there with bitter pools
   Anigh its margin, brushed by heavy trees.
A piping wind the narrow valley cools,
   Fretting the willows and the cypresses.
Gray skies above, and in the gloomy space
An awful presence hath its dwelling-place.

I saw a youth pass down that vale of tears;
   His head was circled with a crown of thorn,
His form was bowed as by the weight of years,
   His wayworn feet by stones were cut and torn.
His eyes were such as have beheld the sword
Of terror of the angel of the Lord.

He passed, and clouds and shadows and thick
     haze
   Fell and encompassed him. I might not see
What hand upheld him in those dismal ways,
   Wherethrough he staggered with his misery.
The creeping mists that trooped and spread
     around,
The smitten head and writhing form enwound.

Then slow and gradual but sure they rose,
   Those clinging vapors blotting out the sky.
The youth had fallen not, his viewless foes
   Discomfited, had left the victory

Unto the heart that fainted not nor failed,
But from the hill-tops its salvation hailed.

I looked at him in dread lest I should see,
    The anguish of the struggle in his eyes ;
And lo, great peace was there !   Triumphantly
    The sunshine crowned him from the sacred
        skies.
" From strength to strength he goes," he leaves
        beneath
The valley of the shadow and of death.

" Thrice blest who passing through that vale of
        Tears,
Makes it a well," — and draws life - nourish-
        ment
From those death-bitter drops. No grief, no
        fears
    Assail him further, he may scorn the event.
For naught hath power to swerve the steadfast
        soul
Within that valley broken and made whole.

THE BANNER OF THE JEW.

WAKE, Israel, wake !   Recall to-day
    The glorious Maccabean rage,
The sire heroic, hoary-gray,
    His five-fold lion-lineage :

The Wise, the Elect, the Help-of-God,
The Burst-of-Spring, the Avenging Rod.[1]

From Mizpeh's mountain-ridge they saw
   Jerusalem's empty streets, her shrine
Laid waste where Greeks profaned the Law,
   With idol and with pagan sign.
Mourners in tattered black were there,
With ashes sprinkled on their hair.

Then from the stony peak there rang
   A blast to ope the graves: down poured
The Maccabean clan, who sang
   Their battle-anthem to the Lord.
Five heroes lead, and following, see,
Ten thousand rush to victory!

Oh for Jerusalem's trumpet now,
   To blow a blast of shattering power,
To wake the sleepers high and low,
   And rouse them to the urgent hour!
No hand for vengeance — but to save,
A million naked swords should wave.

Oh deem not dead that martial fire,
   Say not the mystic flame is spent!
With Moses' law and David's lyre,
   Your ancient strength remains unbent.

[1] The sons of Mattathias — Jonathan, John, Eleazar,
Simon (also called the Jewel), and Judas, the Prince.

Let but an Ezra rise anew,
To lift the *Banner of the Jew!*

A rag, a mock at first — erelong,
  When men have bled and women wept,
To guard its precious folds from wrong,
  Even they who shrunk, even they who slept,
Shall leap to bless it, and to save.
Strike ! for the brave revere the brave !

THE GUARDIAN OF THE RED DISK.

SPOKEN BY A CITIZEN OF MALTA — 1300.

A CURIOUS title held in high repute,
One among many honors, thickly strewn
On my lord Bishop's head, his grace of Malta.
Nobly he bears them all, — with tact, skill, zeal,
Fulfills each special office, vast or slight,
Nor slurs the least minutia, — therewithal
Wears such a stately aspect of command,
Broad-cheeked, broad-chested, reverend, sancti-
      fied,
Haloed with white about the tonsure's rim,
With dropped lids o'er the piercing Spanish eyes
(Lynx-keen, I warrant, to spy out heresy) ;
Tall, massive form, o'ertowering all in presence,
Or ere they kneel to kiss the large white hand.
His looks sustain his deeds, — the perfect pre-
      late,
Whose void chair shall be taken, but not filled.

You know not, who are foreign to the isle,
Haply, what this Red Disk may be, he guards.
'T is the bright blotch, big as the Royal seal,
Branded beneath the beard of every Jew.
These vermin so infest the isle, so slide
Into all byways, highways that may lead
Direct or roundabout to wealth or power,
Some plain, plump mark was needed, to protect
From the degrading contact Christian folk.

The evil had grown monstrous : certain Jews
Wore such a haughty air, had so refined,
With super-subtile arts, strict, monkish lives,
And studious habit, the coarse Hebrew type,
One might have elbowed in the public mart
Iscariot, — nor suspected one's soul-peril.
Christ's blood ! it sets my flesh a-creep to think !
We may breathe freely now, not fearing taint,
Praised be our good Lord Bishop ! He keeps
          count
Of every Jew, and prints on cheek or chin
The scarlet stamp of separateness, of shame.

No beard, blue-black, grizzled or Judas-colored,
May hide that damning little wafer-flame.
When one appears therewith, the urchins know
Good sport's at hand ; they fling their stones and
          mud,
Sure of their game.   But most the wisdom shows
Upon the unbelievers' selves ; they learn

Their proper rank; crouch, cringe, and hide, —
        lay by
Their insolence of self-esteem; no more
Flaunt forth in rich attire, but in dull weeds,
Slovenly donned, would slink past unobserved;
Bow servile necks and crook obsequious knees,
Chin sunk in hollow chest, eyes fixed on earth
Or blinking sidewise, but to apprehend
Whether or not the hated spot be spied.
I warrant my Lord Bishop has full hands,
Guarding the Red Disk — lest one rogue escape!

THE NEW EZEKIEL.

WHAT, can these dead bones live, whose sap is
        dried
    By twenty scorching centuries of wrong?
Is this the House of Israel, whose pride
    Is as a tale that's told, an ancient song?
Are these ignoble relics all that live
    Of psalmist, priest, and prophet? Can the
        breath
Of very heaven bid these bones revive,
    Open the graves and clothe the ribs of death?

Yea, Prophesy, the Lord hath said. Again
    Say to the wind, Come forth and breathe
        afresh,
Even that they may live upon these slain,
    And bone to bone shall leap, and flesh to flesh.

The Spirit is not dead, proclaim the word,
  Where lay dead bones, a host of armed men
    stand !
I ope your graves, my people, saith the Lord,
  And I shall place you living in your land.

THE CHOICE.

I saw in dream the spirits unbegot,
Veiled, floating phantoms, lost in twilight space;
For one the hour had struck, he paused ; the place
Rang with an awful Voice :

                    " Soul, choose thy lot !
Two paths are offered ; that, in velvet-flower,
Slopes easily to every earthly prize.
Follow the multitude and bind thine eyes,
Thou and thy sons' sons shall have peace with
    power.
This narrow track skirts the abysmal verge,
Here shalt thou stumble, totter, weep and bleed,
All men shall hate and hound thee and thy seed,
Thy portion be the wound, the stripe, the scourge.
But in thy hand I place my lamp for light,
Thy blood shall be the witness of my Law,
Choose now for all the ages ! "

                        Then I saw
The unveiled spirit, grown divinely bright,
Choose the grim path. He turned, I knew full well
The pale, great martyr-forehead shadowy-curled,
The glowing eyes that had renounced the world,
Disgraced, despised, immortal Israel.

THE WORLD'S JUSTICE.

IF the sudden tidings came
  That on some far, foreign coast,
Buried ages long from fame,
  Had been found a remnant lost
Of that hoary race who dwelt
  By the golden Nile divine,
Spake the Pharaoh's tongue and knelt
  At the moon-crowned Isis' shrine —
How at reverend Egypt's feet,
Pilgrims from all lands would meet!

If the sudden news were known,
  That anigh the desert-place
Where once blossomed Babylon,
  Scions of a mighty race
Still survived, of giant build,
  Huntsmen, warriors, priest and sage,
Whose ancestral fame had filled,
  Trumpet-tongued, the earlier age,
How at old Assyria's feet
Pilgrims from all lands would meet!

Yet when Egypt's self was young,
  And Assyria's bloom unworn,
Ere the mythic Homer sung,
  Ere the gods of Greece were born,
Lived the nation of one God,
  Priests of freedom, sons of Shem,

Never quelled by yoke or rod,
   Founders of Jerusalem —
Is there one abides to-day,
Seeker of dead cities, say!

Answer, now as then, *they are;*
   Scattered broadcast o'er the lands,
Knit in spirit nigh and far,
   With indissoluble bands.
Half the world adores their God,
   They the living law proclaim,
And their guerdon is — the rod,
   Stripes and scourgings, death and shame.
Still on Israel's head forlorn,
Every nation heaps its scorn.

THE SUPREME SACRIFICE.

WELL-NIGH two thousand years hath Israel
   Suffered the scorn of man for love of God;
   Endured the outlaw's ban, the yoke, the rod,
With perfect patience.   Empires rose and fell,
   Around him Nebo was adored and Bel;
Edom was drunk with victory, and trod
On his high places, while the sacred sod
   Was desecrated by the infidel.
His faith proved steadfast, without breach or flaw,
   But now the last renouncement is required.
His truth prevails, his God is God, his Law
   Is found the wisdom most to be desired.

Not his the glory !   He, maligned, misknown,
Bows his meek head, and says, " Thy will be
    done ! "

THE FEAST OF LIGHTS.

KINDLE the taper like the steadfast star
    Ablaze on evening's forehead o'er the earth,
And add each night a lustre till afar
    An eightfold splendor shine above thy hearth.
Clash, Israel, the cymbals, touch the lyre,
    Blow the brass trumpet and the harsh-tongued
        horn ;
Chant psalms of victory till the heart takes fire,
    The Maccabean spirit leap new-born.

Remember how from wintry dawn till night,
    Such songs were sung in Zion, when again
On the high altar flamed the sacred light,
    And, purified from every Syrian stain,
The foam-white walls with golden shields were
        hung,
    With crowns and silken spoils, and at the
        shrine,
Stood, midst their conqueror-tribe, five chieftains
        sprung
    From one heroic stock, one seed divine.

Five branches grown from Mattathias' stem,
    The Blessed John, the Keen-Eyed Jonathan,

Simon the fair, the Burst-of Spring, the Gem,
  Eleazar, Help of-God; o'er all his clan
Judas the Lion-Prince, the Avenging Rod,
  Towered in warrior-beauty, uncrowned king,
Armed with the breastplate and the sword of God,
  Whose praise is : " He received the perishing."

They who had camped within the mountain-pass,
  Couched on the rock, and tented neath the sky,
Who saw from Mizpah's heights the tangled grass
  Choke the wide Temple-courts, the altar lie
Disfigured and polluted — who had flung
  Their faces on the stones, and mourned aloud
And rent their garments, wailing with one tongue,
  Crushed as a wind-swept bed of reeds is bowed,

Even they by one voice fired, one heart of flame,
  Though broken reeds, had risen, and were
      men,
They rushed upon the spoiler and o'ercame,
  Each arm for freedom had the strength of ten.
Now is their mourning into dancing turned,
  Their sackcloth doffed for garments of delight,
Week-long the festive torches shall be burned,
  Music and revelry wed day with night.

Still ours the dance, the feast, the glorious Psalm,
  The mystic lights of emblem, and the Word.
Where is our Judas? Where our five-branched
      palm ?
  Where are the lion-warriors of the Lord ?

Clash, Israel, the cymbals, touch the lyre,
    Sound the brass trumpet and the harsh-tongued
        horn,
Chant hymns of victory till the heart take fire,
    The Maccabean spirit leap new-born !

GIFTS.

"O World-God, give me Wealth !" the Egyptian
    cried.
His prayer was granted. High as heaven, behold
Palace and Pyramid ; the brimming tide
Of lavish Nile washed all his land with gold.
Armies of slaves toiled ant-wise at his feet,
World-circling traffic roared through mart and
        street,
His priests were gods, his spice-balmed kings en-
    shrined,
Set death at naught in rock-ribbed charnels deep.
Seek Pharaoh's race to-day and ye shall find
Rust and the moth, silence and dusty sleep.

"O World-God, give me beauty !" cried the
        Greek.
His prayer was granted. All the earth became
Plastic and vocal to his sense ; each peak,
Each grove, each stream, quick with Promethean
        flame,
Peopled the world with imaged grace and light.
The lyre was his, and his the breathing might

Of the immortal marble, his the play
Of diamond-pointed thought and golden tongue.
Go seek the sun-shine race, ye find to-day
A broken column and a lute unstrung.

"O World-God, give me Power!" the Roman
    cried.
His prayer was granted. The vast world was
    chained
A captive to the chariot of his pride.
The blood of myriad provinces was drained
To feed that fierce, insatiable red heart.
Invulnerably bulwarked every part
With serried legions and with close-meshed Code,
Within, the burrowing worm had gnawed its home,
A roofless ruin stands where once abode
The imperial race of everlasting Rome.

"O Godhead, give me Truth!" the Hebrew cried.
His prayer was granted; he became the slave
Of the Idea, a pilgrim far and wide,
Cursed, hated, spurned, and scourged with none
    to save.
The Pharaohs knew him, and when Greece be-
    held,
His wisdom wore the hoary crown of Eld.
Beauty he hath forsworn, and wealth and power.
Seek him to-day, and find in every land.
No fire consumes him, neither floods devour;
Immortal through the lamp within his hand.

BAR KOCHBA.

WEEP, Israel! your tardy meed outpour
  Of grateful homage on his fallen head,
That never coronal of triumph wore,
  Untombed, dishonored, and unchapleted.
If Victory makes the hero, raw Success
  The stamp of virtue, unremembered
Be then the desperate strife, the storm and stress
  Of the last Warrior Jew.   But if the man
Who dies for freedom, loving all things less,
  Against world-legions, mustering his poor clan;
The weak, the wronged, the miserable, to send
  Their death-cry's protest through the ages'
    span —
If such an one be worthy, ye shall lend
  Eternal thanks to him, eternal praise.
Nobler the conquered than the conqueror's end!

1492.

THOU two-faced year, Mother of Change and Fate,
Didst weep when Spain cast forth with flaming
    sword,
The children of the prophets of the Lord,
Prince, priest, and people, spurned by zealot hate.
Hounded from sea to sea, from state to state,
The West refused them, and the East abhorred.
No anchorage the known world could afford,
Close-locked was every port, barred every gate.

Then smiling, thou unveil'dst, O two-faced
    year,
A virgin world where doors of sunset part,
Saying,   "Ho, all who weary, enter here !
There falls each ancient barrier that the art
Of race or creed or rank devised, to rear
Grim bulwarked hatred between heart and heart !"
  1883.

THE BIRTH OF MAN.

A LEGEND OF THE TALMUD.

I.

WHEN angels visit earth, the messengers
Of God's decree, they come as lightning, wind :
Before the throne, they all are living fire.
There stand four rows of angels — to the right
The hosts of Michael, Gabriel's to the left,
Before, the troop of Ariel, and behind,
The ranks of Raphael ; all, with one accord,
Chanting the glory of the Everlasting.
Upon the high and holy throne there rests,
Invisible, the Majesty of God.
About his brows the crown of mystery
Whereon the sacred letters are engraved
Of the unutterable Name.   He grasps
A sceptre of keen fire ; the universe
Is compassed in His glance ; at His right hand
Life stands, and at His left hand standeth Death.

II.

Lo, the divine idea of making man
Had spread abroad among the heavenly hosts;
And all at once before the immortal throne
Pressed troops of angels and of seraphim,
With minds opposed, and contradicting cries:
"Fulfill, great Father, thine exalted thought!
Create and give unto the earth her king!"
"Cease, cease, Almighty God! create no more!"
And suddenly upon the heavenly sphere
Deep silence fell; before the immortal throne
The angel Mercy knelt, and thus he spoke:
"Fulfill, great Father, thine exalted thought!
Create the likeness of thyself on earth.
In this new creature I will breathe the spirit
Of a divine compassion; he shall be
Thy fairest image in the universe."
But to his words the angel Peace replied,
With heavy sobs: "My spirit was outspread,
Oh God, on thy creation, and all things
Were sweetly bound in gracious harmony.
But man, this strange new being, everywhere
Shall bring confusion, trouble, discord, war."
"Avenger of injustice and of crime,"
Exclaimed the angel Justice, "he shall be
Subject to me, and peace shall bloom again.
Create, oh Lord, create!" "Father of truth,"
Implored with tears the angel Truth, "Thou
        bring'st

Upon the earth the father of all lies ! "
And over the celestial faces gloomed
A cloud of grief, and stillness deep prevailed.
Then from the midst of that abyss of light
Whence sprang the eternal throne, these words
    rang forth :
" Be comforted, my daughter !   Thee I send
To be companion unto man on earth."
And all the angels cried, lamenting loud :
" Thou robbest heaven of her fairest gem.
Truth ! seal of all thy thoughts, Almighty God,
The richest jewel that adorns thy crown."
From the abyss of glory rang the voice :
" From heaven to earth, from earth once more to
    heaven,
Shall Truth, with constant interchange, alight
And soar again, an everlasting link
Between the world and sky."
        And man was born.

RASCHI IN PRAGUE.

RASCHI OF TROYES, the Moon of Israel,
The authoritative Talmudist, returned
From his wide wanderings under many skies,
To all the synagogues of the Orient,
Through Spain and Italy, the isles of Greece,
Beautiful, dolorous, sacred Palestine,
Dead, obelisked Egypt, floral, musk - breathed
    Persia,

Laughing with bloom, across the Caucasus,
The interminable sameness of bare steppes,
Through dark luxuriance of Bohemian woods,
And issuing on the broad, bright Moldau vale,
Entered the gates of Prague. Here, too, his
      fame,
Being winged, preceded him. His people
      swarmed
Like bees to gather the rich honey-dew
Of learning from his lips. Amazement filled
All eyes beholding him. No hoary sage,
He who had sat in Egpyt at the feet
Of Moses ben-Maimuni, called him friend;
Raschi the scholiast, poet, and physician,
Who bore the ponderous Bible's storied wis-
      dom,
The Mischna's tangled lore at tip of tongue,
Light as a garland on a lance, appeared
In the just-ripened glory of a man.
From his clear eye youth flamed magnificent;
Force, masked by grace, moved in his balanced
      frame;
An intellectual, virile beauty reigned
Dominant on domed brow, on fine, firm lips,
An eagle profile cut in gilded bronze,
Strong, delicate as a head upon a coin,
While, as an aureole crowns a burning lamp,
Above all beauty of the body and brain
Shone beauty of a soul benign with love.
Even as a tawny flock of huddled sheep,

Grazing each other's heels, urged by one will,
With bleat and baa following the wether's lead,
Or the wise shepherd, so o'er the Moldau bridge
Trotted the throng of yellow-caftaned Jews,
Chattering, hustling, shuffling. At their head
Marched Rabbi Jochanan ben-Eleazar,
High priest in Prague, oldest and most revered,
To greet the star of Israel. As a father
Yearns toward his son, so toward the noble
     Raschi
Leapt at first sight the patriarch's fresh old heart.
" My home be thine in Prague ! Be thou my
     son,
Who have no offspring save one simple girl.
See, glorious youth, who dost renew the days
Of David and of Samuel, early graced
With God's anointing oil, how Israel
Delights to honor who hath honored him."
Then Raschi, though he felt a ball of fire
Globe itself in his throat, maintained his calm,
His cheek's opaque, swart pallor while he kissed
Silent the Rabbi's withered hand, and bowed
Divinely humble, his exalted head
Craving the benison.

              For each who asked
He had the word of counsel, comfort, help ;
For all, rich eloquence of thanks. His voice,
Even and grave, thrilled secret chords and set
Plain speech to music. Certain folk were there
Sick in the body, dragging painful limbs,

To the physician.   These he solaced first,
With healing touch, with simples from his pouch,
Warming and lulling, best with promises
Of constant service till their ills were cured.
And some, gray-bearded, bald, and curved with
      age,
Blear-eyed from poring over lines obscure
And knotty riddles of the Talmud, brought
Their problems to this youth, who cleared and
      solved,
Yielding prompt answer to a lifetime's search.
Then, followed, pushed by his obsequious tribe,
Who fain had pedestaled him on their backs,
Hemming his steps, choking the airs of heaven
With their oppressive honors, he advanced,
Midst shouts, tumultuous welcomes, kisses show-
      ered
Upon his road-stained garments, through Prague's
      streets,
Gaped at by Gentiles, hissed at and reviled,
But no whit altering his majestic mien
For overwhelming plaudits or contempt.
Glad tidings Raschi brought from West and East
Of thriving synagogues, of famous men,
And flourishing academies.   In Rome
The Papal treasurer was a pious Jew,
Rabbi Jehiel, neath whose patronage
Prospered a noble school.   Two hundred Jews
Dwelt free and paid no tributary mark.
Three hundred lived in peace at Capua,

Shepherded by the learned Rabbi David,
A prince of Israel.   In Babylon
The Jews established their Academy.
Another still in Bagdad, from whose chair
Preached the great rabbi, Samuel Ha-levi,
Versed in the written and the oral law,
Who blindfold could repeat the whole vast text
Of Mischna and Gemara.   On the banks
Of Eden-born Euphrates, one day's ride
From Bagdad, Raschi found in the wilderness,
Which once was Babylon, Ezekiel's tomb.
Thrice ten perpetual lamps starred the dim
      shrine,
Two hundred sentinels held the sleepless vigil,
Receiving offerings.   At the Feast of Booths
Here crowded Jews by thousands, out of Persia,
From all the neighboring lands, to celebrate
The glorious memories of the golden days.
Ten thousand Jews with their Academy
Damascus boasted, while in Cairo shone
The pearl, the crown of Israel, ben-Maimuni,
Physician at the Court of Saladin,
The second Moses, gathering at his feet
Sages from all the world.

              As Raschi spake,
Forgetting or ignoring the chief shrine,
The Exile's Home, whereunto yearned all hearts,
All ears were strained for tidings.   Some one
      asked:
" What of Jerusalem ?   Speak to us of Zion."

The light died from his eyes.   From depths pro-
      found
Issued his grave, great voice : " Alas for Zion !
Verily is she fallen !   Where our race
Dictated to the nations, not a handful,
Nay, not a score, not ten, not two abide !
One, only one, one solitary Jew,
The Rabbi Abraham Haceba, flits
Ghostlike amid the ruins ; every year
Beggars himself to pay the idolaters
The costly tax for leave to hold a-gape
His heart's live wound ; to weep, a mendicant,
Amidst the crumbled stones of palaces
Where reigned his ancestors, upon the graves
Where sleep the priests, the prophets, and the
      kings
Who were his forefathers.   Ask me no more ! "

Now, when the French Jew's advent was pro-
      claimed,
And his tumultuous greeting, envious growls
And ominous eyebeams threatened storm in
      Prague.
" Who may this miracle of learning be ?
The Anti-Christ !   The century-long-awaited,
The hourly-hoped Messiah, come at last !
Else dared they never wax so arrogant,
Flaunting their monstrous joy in Christian eyes,
And strutting peacock-like, with hideous screams,
Who are wont to crawl, mute reptiles underfoot."

A stone or two flung at some servile form,
Liveried in the yellow gaberdine
(With secret happiness but half suppressed
On features cast for misery), served at first
For chance expression of the rabble's hate;
But, swelling like a snow-ball rolled along
By mischief-plotting boys, the rage increased,
Grew to a mighty mass, until it reached
The palace of Duke Vladislaw.   He heard
With righteous wrath his injured subjects' charge
Against presumptuous aliens: how these blocked
His avenues, his bridges; bared to the sun
The canker-taint of Prague's obscurest coigne;
Paraded past the churches of the Lord
One who denied Him, one by them hailed Christ.
Enough! This cloud, no bigger than one's hand,
Gains overweening bulk.   Prague harbored, first,
Out of contemptuous ruth, a wretched band
Of outcast paupers, gave them leave to ply
Their money-lending trade, and leased them land
On all too facile terms.   Behold! to-day,
Like leeches bloated with the people's blood,
They batten on Bohemia's poverty;
They breed and grow; like adders, spit back hate
And venomed perfidy for Christian love.
Thereat the Duke, urged by wise counsellors —
Narzerad the statesman (half whose wealth was pledged
To the usurers), abetted by the priest,

Bishop of Olmütz, who had visited
The Holy Sepulchre, whose long, full life
Was one clean record of pure piety —
The Duke, I say, by these persuasive tongues,
Coaxed to his darling aim, forbade his guards
To hinder the just anger of his town,
And ordered to be led in chains to him
The pilgrim and his host.

                            At noontide meal
Raschi sat, full of peace, with Jochanan,
And the sole daughter of the house, Rebekah,
Young, beautiful as her namesake when she
      brought
Her firm, frail pitcher balanced on her neck
Unto the well, and gave the stranger drink,
And gave his camels drink. The servant set
The sparkling jar's refreshment from his lips,
And saw the virgin's face, bright as the moon,
Beam from the curled luxuriance of black locks,
And cast-back linen veil's soft-folded cloud,
Then put the golden ear-ring by her cheek,
The bracelets on her hands, his master's pledge,
Isaac's betrothal gift, whom she should wed,
And be the mother of millions — one whose seed
Dwells in the gates of those which hate them.
                                   So
Yearned Raschi to adorn the radiant girl
Who sat at board before him, nor dared lift
Shy, heavy lids from pupils black as grapes

That dart the imprisoned sunshine from their
    core.
But in her ears keen sense was born to catch,
And in her heart strange power to hold, each
    tone
O' the low-keyed, vibrant voice, each syllable
O' the eloquent discourse, enriched with tales
Of venturous travel, brilliant with fine points
Of delicate humor, or illustrated
With living portraits of world-famoused men,
Jews, Saracens, Crusaders, Islamites,
Whose hand he had grasped — the iron warrior,
Godfrey of Bouillon, the wise infidel
Who in all strength, wit, courtesy excelled
The kings his foes — imperial Saladin.
But even as Raschi spake an abrupt noise
Of angry shouts, of battering staves that shook
The oaken portal, stopped the enchanted voice,
The uplifted wine spilled from the nerveless
    hand
Of Rabbi Jochanan. " God pity us!
Our enemies are upon us once again.
Hie thee, Rebekah, to the inmost chamber,
Far from their wanton eyes' polluting gaze,
Their desecrating touch! Kiss me! Begone!
Raschi, my guest, my son " — But no word more
Uttered the reverend man. With one huge
    crash
The strong doors split asunder, pouring in
A stream of soldiers, ruffians, armed with pikes,

Lances, and clubs — the unchained beast, the
    mob.
" Behold the town's new guest ! " jeered one who
    tossed
The half-filled golden wine-cup's contents straight
In the noble pure young face. "What, master
    Jew !
Must your good friends of Prague break bolts
    and bars
To gain a peep at this prodigious pearl
You bury in your shell ?   Forth to the day !
Our Duke himself claims share of your new
    wealth ;
Summons to court the Jew philosopher ! "
Then, while some stuffed their pokes with baubles
    snatched
From board and shelf, or with malignant sword
Slashed the rich Orient rugs, the pictured woof
That clothed the wall ; others had seized and
    bound,
And gagged from speech, the helpless, aged man ;
Still others outraged, with coarse, violent hands,
The marble-pale, rigid as stone, strange youth,
Whose eye like struck flint flashed, whose nether
    lip
Was threaded with a scarlet line of blood,
Where the compressed teeth fixed it to forced
    calm.
He struggled not while his free limbs were tied,
His beard plucked, torn and spat upon his robe —

Seemed scarce to know these insults were for
      him ;
But never swerved his gaze from Jochanan.
Then, in God's language, sealed from these dumb
      brutes,
Swiftly and low he spake : " Be of good cheer,
Reverend old man. I deign not treat with these.
If one dare offer bodily hurt to thee,
By the ineffable Name ! I snap my chains
Like gossamer, and in his blood, to the hilt,
Bathe the prompt knife hid in my girdle's folds.
The Duke shall hear me. Patience. Trust in
      me."
Somewhat the authoritative voice abashed,
Even hoarse and changed, the miscreants, who
      feared
Some strong curse lurked in this mysterious
      tongue,
Armed with this evil eye.   But brief the spell.
With gibe and scoff they dragged their victims
      forth,
The abused old man, the proud, insulted youth,
O'er the late path of his triumphal march,
Befouled with mud, with raiment torn, wild hair
And ragged beard, to Vladislaw. He sat
Expectant in his cabinet. On one side
His secular adviser, Narzerad,
Quick-eyed, sharp-nosed, red-whiskered as a fox ;
On the other hand his spiritual guide,
Bishop of Olmütz, unctuous, large, and bland.

" So these twain are chief culprits ! " sneered the
       Duke,
Measuring with the noble's ignorant scorn
His masters of a lesser caste.   " Stand forth !
Rash, stubborn, vain old man, whose impudence
Hath choked the public highways with thy brood
Of nasty vermin, by our sufferance hid
In lanes obscure, who hailed this charlatan
With sky-flung caps, bent knees, and echoing
       shouts,
Due to ourselves alone in Prague ; yea, worse,
Who offered worship even ourselves disclaim,
Our Lord Christ's meed, to this blaspheming
       Jew —
Thy crimes have murdered patience.   Thou hast
       wrecked
Thy people's fortune with thy own.   But first
(For even in anger we are just) recount
With how great compensation from thy store
Of hoarded gold and jewels thou wilt buy
Remission of the penalty.   Be wise.
Hark how my subjects, storming through the
       streets,
Vent on thy tribe accursed their well-based
       wrath."
And, truly, through closed casements roared the
       noise
Of mighty surging crowds, derisive cries,
And victims' screams of anguish and affright.
Then Raschi, royal in his rags, began :

"Hear me, my liege!" At that commanding
    voice,
The Bishop, who with dazed eyes had perused
The grieved, wise, beautiful, pale face, sprang
    up,
Quick recognition in his glance, warm joy
Aflame on his broad cheeks. "No more! No
    more!
Thou art the man! Give me the hand to kiss
That raised me from the shadow of the grave
In Jaffa's lazar-house! Listen, my liege!
During my pilgrimage to Palestine
I, sickened with the plague and nigh to death,
Languished 'midst strangers, all my crumbling
    flesh
One rotten mass of sores, a thing for dogs
To shy from, shunned by Christian as by Turk,
When lo! this clean-breathed, pure-souled,
    blessed youth,
Whom I, not knowing for an infidel,
Seeing featured like the Christ, believed a saint,
Sat by my pillow, charmed the sting from pain,
Quenched the fierce fever's heat, defeated Death;
And when I was made whole, had disappeared,
No man knew whither, leaving no more trace
Than a re-risen angel. This is he!"
Then Raschi, who had stood erect, nor quailed
From glances of hot hate or crazy wrath,
Now sank his eagle gaze, stooped his high head,
Veiling his glowing brow, returned the kiss

Of brother-love upon the Christian's hand,
And dropping on his knees implored the three,
" Grace for my tribe!   They are what ye have
        made.
If any be among them fawning, false,
Insatiable, revengeful, ignorant, mean —
And there are many such — ask your own hearts
What virtues ye would yield for planted hate,
Ribald contempt, forced, menial servitude,
Slow centuries of vengeance for a crime
Ye never did commit ?   Mercy for these !
Who bear on back and breast the scathing brand
Of scarlet degradation, who are clothed
In ignominious livery, whose bowed necks
Are broken with the yoke.   Change these to men !
That were a noble witchcraft simply wrought,
God's alchemy transforming clods to gold.
If there be one among them strong and wise,
Whose lips anoint breathe poetry and love,
Whose brain and heart served ever Christian
        need —
And there are many such — for his dear sake,
Lest ye chance murder one of God's high priests,
Spare his thrice-wretched tribe !   Believe me,
        sirs,
Who have seen various lands, searched various
        hearts,
I have yet to touch that undiscovered shore,
Have yet to fathom that impossible soul,
Where a true benefit's forgot; where one

Slight deed of common kindness sown yields not
As now, as here, abundant crop of love.
Every good act of man, our Talmud says,
Creates an angel, hovering by his side.
Oh! what a shining host, great Duke, shall
     guard
Thy consecrated throne, for all the lives
Thy mercy spares, for all the tears thy ruth
Stops at the source. Behold this poor old man,
Last of a line of princes, stricken in years,
As thy dead father would have been to-day.
Was that white beard a rag for obscene hands
To tear? a weed for lumpish clowns to pluck?
Was that benignant, venerable face
Fit target for their foul throats' voided rheum?
That wrinkled flesh made to be pulled and
     pricked,
Wounded by flinty pebbles and keen steel?
Behold the prostrate, patriarchal form,
Bruised, silent, chained. Duke, such is Israel!"
" Unbind these men! " commanded Vladislaw.
" Go forth and still the tumult of my town.
Let no Jew suffer violence. Raschi, rise!
Thou who hast served the Christ — with this
     priest's life,
Who is my spirit's counselor — Christ serves thee.
Return among thy people with my seal,
The talisman of safety. Let them know
The Duke's their friend. Go, publish the glad
     news! "

Raschi the Saviour, Raschi the Messiah,
Back to the Jewry carried peace and love.
But Narzerad fed his venomed heart with gall,
Vowing to give his fatal hatred vent,
Despite a world of weak fantastic Dukes
And heretic bishops.   He fulfilled his vow.

THE DEATH OF RASCHI.

[AARON BEN MEIR *loquitur.*]

IF I remember Raschi?   An I live,
Grandson, to bless thy grandchild, I 'll forget
Never that youth and what he did for Prague.
Aye, aye, I know! he slurred a certain verse
In such and such a prayer; omitted quite
To stand erect there where the ritual
Commands us rise and bow towards the East;
Therefore, the ingrates brand him heterodox,
Neglect his memory whose virtue saved
Each knave of us alive.   Not I forget,
No more does God, who wrought a miracle
For his dear sake.   The Passover was here.
Raschi, just wedded with the fair Rebekah,
Bode but the lapsing of the holy week
For homeward journey with his bride to France.
The sacred meal was spread.   All sat at board
Within the house of Rabbi Jochanan:
The kind old priest; his noble, new-found son,
Whose name was wrung in every key of praise,

By every voice in Prague, from Duke to serf
(Save the vindictive bigot, Narzerad) ;
The beautiful young wife, whose cup of joy
Sparkled at brim ; next her the vacant chair
Awaited the Messiah, who, unannounced,
In God's good time shall take his place with us.
Now when the Rabbi reached the verse where
      one
Shall rise from table, flinging wide the door,
To give the Prophet entrance, if so be
The glorious hour have sounded, Raschi rose,
Pale, grave, yet glad with great expectancy,
Crossed the hushed room, and, with a joyous smile
To greet the Saviour, opened the door.
                   A curse !
A cry, " Revenged ! " a thrust, a stifled moan,
The sheathing of a poniard — that was all !
In the dark vestibule a fleeing form,
Masked, gowned in black ; and in the room of
      prayer,
Raschi, face downward on the stone-cold floor,
Bleeding his life out. Oh! what a cry was that
(Folk shuddered, hearing, roods off in the street)
Wherewith Rebekah rushed to raise her lord,
Kneeling beside him, striving in vain to quench
With turban, veil, torn shreds of gown, stained
      hands,
The black blood's sickening gush. He never
      spoke,
Never rewarded with one glance of life

The passion in her eyes.   He met his end
Even as beneath the sickle the full ear
Bows to its death — so beautiful, silent, ripe.

Well, we poor Jews must gulp our injuries,
Howe'er they choke us.   What redress in Prague
For the inhuman murder?   A strange Jew
The victim; the suspected criminal
The ducal counselor!   Such odds forbade
Revenge or justice.   We forbore to seek.
The priest, discrowned o' the glory of his age,
The widow-bride, mourned as though smitten of
        God,
Gave forth they would with solemn obsequies
Bury their dead, and crave no help from man.
Now of what chanced betwixt the night of mur-
        der
And the appointed burial I can give
Only the sum of gossip — servants' tales,
Neighbors' reports, close confidences leaked
From friends and kindred.   Night and day, folk
        said,
Rebekah wept, prayed, fasted by the corpse,
Three mortal days.   Upon the third, her eyes,
Sunk in their pits, glimmered with wild, strange
        fire.
She started from her place beside the dead,
Kissed clay-cold brow, cheeks, lids, and lips
        once more,
And with a maniac's wan, heart-breaking smile,

Veiled, hooded, glided through the twilight
      streets,
A sable shadow. From the willow-grove,
Close by the Moldau's brink, beyond the bridge,
Her trace was lost. 'T was evening and mild
      May,
Air full of spring, skies perfect as a pearl ;
Yet one who saw her pass amidst the shades
O' the blue-gray branches swears a sudden flame,
As of miraculous lightning, thrilled through
      heaven.
One hour thereafter she reëntered Prague,
Slid swiftly through the streets, as though borne
      on
By ankle-wings or floating on soft cloud,
Smiling no more, but with illumined eyes,
Transfigured brow, grave lips, and faltering
      limbs,
So came into the room where Raschi lay
Stretched 'twixt tall tapers lit at head and foot.
She held in both hands leafy, flowerless plants,
Some she had fastened in her twisted hair,
Stuck others in her girdle, and from all
Issued a racy odor, pungent-sweet,
The living soul of Spring. Death's chamber
      seemed
As though clear sunshine and a singing bird
Therein had entered. From the precious herb
She poured into a golden bowl the sap,
Sparkling like wine ; then with a soundless prayer,

White as the dead herself, she held the cup
To Raschi's mouth.   A quick, small flame sprang
    up
From the enchanted balsam, died away,
And lo! the color dawned in cheek and lips,
The life returned, the sealed, blind lids were
    raised,
And in the glorious eyes love reawoke,
And, looking up, met love.

                  So runs the tale,
Mocked by the worldly-wise; but I believe,
Knowing the miracles the Lord hath wrought
In every age for Jacob's seed.   Moreover,
I, with the highest and meanest Jew in Prague,
Was at the burial.   No man saw the dead.
Sealed was the coffin ere the rites began,
And none could swear it went not empty down
Into the hollow earth.   Too shrewd our priest
To publish such a wonder, and expose
That consecrated life to second death.
Scarce were the thirty days of mourning sped,
When we awoke to find his home left bare,
Rebekah and her father fled from Prague.
God grant they had glad meeting otherwhere!

AN EPISTLE.

FROM JOSHUA IBN VIVES OF ALLORQUI TO HIS FOR-
MER MASTER, SOLOMON LEVI-PAUL, DE SANTA-MARIA,
BISHOP OF CARTAGENA CHANCELLOR OF CASTILE, AND
PRIVY COUNCILLOR TO KING HENRY III. OF SPAIN.

[In this poem I have done little more than elaborate and versify
the account given in Graetz's History of the Jews (Vol. VIII., page
77), of an Epistle actually written in the beginning of the 15th
century by Joshua ben Joseph Ibn Vives to Paulus de Santa Maria
— E. L.] (1).

I.

MASTER and Sage, greetings and health to thee,
   From thy most meek disciple! Deign once
      more
Endure me at thy feet, enlighten me,
   As when upon my boyish head of yore,
Midst the rapt circle gathered round thy knee
   Thy sacred vials of learning thou didst pour.
By the large lustre of thy wisdom orbed
Be my black doubts illumined and absorbed.

II.

Oft I recall that golden time when thou,
   Born for no second station, heldst with us
The Rabbi's chair, who art priest and bishop
      now ;
   And we, the youth of Israel, curious,
Hung on thy counsels, lifted reverent brow
   Unto thy sanctity, would fain discuss

With thee our Talmud problems good and evil,
Till startled by the risen stars o'er Seville.

III.

For on the Synagogue's high-pillared porch
    Thou didst hold session, till the sudden sun
Beyond day's purple limit dropped his torch.
    Then we, as dreamers, woke, to find outrun
Time's rapid sands. The flame that may not
        scorch,
    Our hearts caught from thine eyes, thou Shin-
        ing One.
I scent not yet sweet lemon-groves in flower,
But I re-breathe the peace of that deep hour.

IV.

We kissed the sacred borders of thy gown,
    Brow-aureoled with thy blessing, we went forth
Through the hushed byways of the twilight town.
    Then in all life but one thing seemed of worth,
To seek, find, love the Truth.   She set her crown
    Upon thy head, our Master, at thy birth;
She bade thy lips drop honey, fired thine eyes
With the unclouded glow of sun-steeped skies.

V.

Forgive me, if I dwell on that which, viewed
    From thy new vantage-ground, must seem a
        mist
Of error, by auroral youth endued
    With alien lustre.   Still in me subsist

Those reeking vapors ; faith and gratitude
   Still lead me to the hand my boy-lips kissed
For benison and guidance.   Not in wrath,
Master, but in wise patience, point my path.

VI.

For I, thy servant, gather in one sheaf
   The venomed shafts of slander, which thy word
Shall shrivel to small dust.   If haply grief,
   Or momentary pain, I deal, my Lord
Blame not thy servant's zeal, nor be thou deaf
   Unto my soul's blind cry for light.   Accord —
Pitying my love, if too superb to care
For hate-soiled name — an answer to my prayer.

VII.

To me, who, vine to stone, clung close to thee,
   The very base of life appeared to quake
When first I knew thee fallen from us, to be
   A tower of strength among our foes, to make
'Twixt Jew and Jew deep-cloven enmity.
   I have wept gall and blood for thy dear sake.
But now with temperate soul I calmly search
Motive and cause that bound thee to the Church.

VIII.

Four motives possible therefor I reach —
   Ambition, doubt, fear, or mayhap — conviction.
I hear in turn ascribed thee all and each
   By ignorant folk who part not truth from fic-
     tion.

But I, whom even thyself didst stoop to teach,
　　May poise the scales, weigh this with that con-
　　　　fliction,
Yea, sift the hid grain motive from the dense,
Dusty, eye-blinding chaff of consequence.

IX.

Ambition first!　I find no fleck thereof
　　In all thy clean soul.　What! could glory,
　　　　gold,
Or sated senses lure thy lofty love?
　　No purple cloak to shield thee from the cold,
No jeweled sign to flicker thereabove,
　　And dazzle men to homage — joys untold
Of spiritual treasure, grace divine,
Alone (so saidst thou) coveting for thine!

X.

I saw thee mount with deprecating air,
　　Step after step, unto our Jewish throne
Of supreme dignity, the Rabbi's chair;
　　Shrinking from public honors thrust upon
Thy meek desert, regretting even there
　　The placid habit of thy life foregone;
Silence obscure, vast peace and austere days
Passed in wise contemplation, prayer, and praise.

XI.

One less than thou had ne'er known such regret.
　　How must thou suffer, who so lov'st the shade,

In Fame's full glare, whom one stride more shall
  set
 Upon the Papal seat! I stand dismayed,
Familiar with thy fearful soul, and yet
 Half glad, perceiving modest worth repaid
Even by the Christians! Could thy soul de-
  flect?
No, no, thrice no! Ambition I reject!

XII.

Next doubt. Could doubt have swayed thee,
  then I ask,
 How enters doubt within the soul of man?
Is it a door that opens, or a mask
 That falls? and Truth's resplendent face we
  scan.
Nay, 't is a creeping, small, blind worm, whose
  task
 Is gnawing at Faith's base; the whole vast
  plan
Rots, crumbles, eaten inch by inch within,
And on its ruins falsehood springs and sin.

XIII.

But thee no doubt confused, no problems vexed.
 Thy father's faith for thee proved bright and
  sweet.
Thou foundst no rite superfluous, no text
 Obscure; the path was straight before thy
  feet.

Till thy baptismal day, thou, unperplexed
  By foreign dogma, didst our prayers repeat,
Honor the God of Israel, fast and feast,
Even as thy people's wont, from first to least.

XIV.

Yes, Doubt I likewise must discard.   Not sleek,
  Full-faced, erect of head, men walk, when
      doubt
Writhes at their entrails; pinched and lean of
      cheek,
  With brow pain-branded, thou hadst strayed
      about
As midst live men a ghost condemned to seek
  That soul he may nor live nor die without.
No doubts the font washed from thee, thou didst
      glide
From creed to creed, complete, sane-souled, clear-
      eyed.

XV.

Thy pardon, Master, if I dare sustain
  The thesis thou couldst entertain a fear.
I would but rout thine enemies, who feign
  Ignoble impulse prompted thy career.
I will but weigh the chances and make plain
  To Envy's self the monstrous jest appear.
Though time, place, circumstance confirmed in
      seeming,
One word from thee should frustrate all their
      scheming.

XVI.

Was Israel glad in Seville on the day
   Thou didst renounce him? Then mightst thou
      indeed
Snap finger at whate'er thy slanderers say.
   Lothly must I admit, just then the seed
Of Jacob chanced upon a grievous way.
   Still from the wounds of that red year we
      bleed.
The curse had fallen upon our heads — the
      sword
Was whetted for the chosen of the Lord.

XVII.

There where we flourished like a fruitful palm,
   We were uprooted, spoiled, lopped limb from
      limb.
A bolt undreamed of out of heavens calm,
   So cracked our doom. We were destroyed by
      him
Whose hand since childhood we had clasped.
      With balm
   Our head had been anointed, at the brim
Our cup ran over — now our day was done,
Our blood flowed free as water in the sun.

XVIII.

Midst the four thousand of our tribe who held
   Glad homes in Seville, never a one was spared,

Some slaughtered at their hearthstones, some ex-
  pelled
 To Moorish slavery. Cunningly ensnared,
Baited and trapped were we ; their fierce monks
  yelled
 And thundered from our Synagogues, while
  flared
The Cross above the Ark. Ah, happiest they
Who fell unconquered martyrs on that day !

XIX.

For some (I write it with flushed cheek, bowed
  head),
 Given free choice 'twixt death and shame, chose
  shame,
Denied the God who visibly had led
 Their fathers, pillared in a cloud of flame,
Bathed in baptismal waters, ate the bread
 Which is their new Lord's body, took the name
Marranos the Accursed, whom equally
Jew, Moor, and Christian hate, despise, and flee.

XX.

Even one no less than an Abarbanel
 Prized miserable length of days, above
Integrity of soul. Midst such who fell,
 Far be it, however, from my duteous love,
Master, to reckon thee. Thine own lips tell
 How fear nor torture thy firm will could move.
How thou midst panic nowise disconcerted,
By Thomas of Aquinas wast converted !

XXI.

Truly I know no more convincing way
  To read so wise an author, than was thine.
When burning Synagogues changed night to day,
    And red swords underscored each word and
      line.
That was a light to read by! Who 'd gainsay
    Authority so clearly stamped divine ?
On this side, death and torture, flame and
      slaughter,
On that, a harmless wafer and clean water.

XXII.

Thou couldst not fear extinction for our race ;
    Though Christian sword and fire from town to
      town
Flash double bladed lightning to efface
    Israel's image — though we bleed, burn, drown
Through Christendom — 't is but a scanty space.
    Still are the Asian hills and plains our own,
Still are we lords in Syria, still are free,
Nor doomed to be abolished utterly.

XXIII.

One sole conclusion hence at last I find,
    Thou whom ambition, doubt, nor fear could
      swerve,
Perforce hast been persuaded through the mind,
    Proved, tested the new dogmas, found them
      serve

Thy spirit's needs, left flesh and sense behind,
   Accepted without shrinking or reserve,
The trans-substantial bread and wine, the Christ
At whose shrine thine own kin were sacrificed.

XXIV.

Here then the moment comes when I crave light.
   All 's dark to me.   Master, if I be blind,
Thou shalt unseal my lids and bless with sight,
   Or groping in the shadows, I shall find
Whether within me or without, dwell night.
   Oh cast upon my doubt-bewildered mind
One ray from thy clear heaven of sun-bright faith,
Grieving, not wroth, at what thy servant saith.

XXV.

Where are the signs fulfilled whereby all men
   Should know the Christ?   Where is the wide-
      winged peace
Shielding the lamb within the lion's den?
   The freedom broadening with the wars that
      cease?
Do foes clasp hands in brotherhood again?
   Where is the promised garden of increase,
When like a rose the wilderness should bloom?
Earth is a battlefield and Spain a tomb.

XXVI.

Our God of Sabaoth is an awful God
   Of lightnings and of vengeance, — Christians
      say.

Earth trembled, nations perished at his nod;
　His Law has yielded to a milder sway.
Theirs is the God of Love whose feet have trod
　　Our common earth — draw near to him and
　　　pray,
Meek-faced, dove-eyed, pure-browed, the Lord of
　　life,
Know him and kneel, else at your throat the
　　knife!

XXVII.

This is the God of Love, whose altars reek
　With human blood, who teaches men to hate;
Torture past words, or sins we may not speak
　　Wrought by his priests behind the convent-
　　　grate.
Are his priests false? or are his doctrines weak
　　That none obeys him? State at war with
　　　state,
Church against church — yea, Pope at feud with
　　Pope
In these tossed seas what anchorage for hope?

XXVIII.

Not only for the sheep without the fold
　Is the knife whetted, who refuse to share
Blessings the shepherd wise doth not withhold
　　Even from the least among his flock — but
　　　there
Midmost the pale, dissensions manifold,
　　Lamb flaying lamb, fierce sheep that rend and
　　　tear.

Master, if thou to thy pride's goal should come,
Where wouldst thou throne — at Avignon or
    Rome ?

XXIX.

I handle burning questions, good my lord,
    Such as may kindle fagots, well I wis.
Your Gospel not denies our older Word,
    But in a way completes and betters this.
The Law of Love shall supersede the sword,
    So runs the promise, but the facts I miss.
Already needs this wretched generation,
A voice divine — a new, third revelation.

XXX.

Two Popes and their adherents fulminate
    Ban against ban, and to the nether hell
Condemn each other, while the nations wait
    Their Christ to thunder forth from Heaven,
        and tell
Who is his rightful Vicar, reinstate
    His throne, the hideous discord to dispel.
Where shall I seek, master, while such things be,
Celestial truth, revealed certainty !

XXXI.

Not miracles I doubt, for how dare man,
    Chief miracle of life's mystery, say *he knows?*
How may he closely secret causes scan,
    Who learns not whence he comes nor where
        he goes ?

Like one who walks in sleep a doubtful span
   He gropes through all his days, till Death un-
      close
His cheated eyes and in one blinding gleam,
Wakes, to discern the substance from the dream.

XXXII.

I say not therefore I deny the birth,
   The Virgin's motherhood, the resurrection,
Who know not how mine own soul came to earth,
   Nor what shall follow death.   Man's imperfec-
      tion
May bound not even in thought the height and
      girth
   Of God's omnipotence ; neath his direction
We may approach his essence, but that He
Should dwarf Himself to us — it cannot be !

XXXIII.[1]

The God who balances the clouds, who spread
   The sky above us like a molten glass,
The God who shut the sea with doors, who laid
   The corner-stone of earth, who caused the
      grass
Spring forth upon the wilderness, and made
   The darkness scatter and the night to pass —
That He should clothe Himself with flesh, and
      move
Midst worms a worm — this, sun, moon, stars
      disprove.

        The Book of Job.[1]

XXXIV.

Help me, O thou who wast my boyhood's guide,
    I bend my exile-weary feet to thee,
Teach me the indivisible to divide,
    Show me how three are one and One is three!
How Christ to save all men was crucified,
    Yet I and mine are damned eternally.
Instruct me, Sage, why Virtue starves alone,
While falsehood step by step ascends the throne.

BY THE WATERS OF BABYLON.

LITTLE POEMS IN PROSE.

I. THE EXODUS.   (AUGUST 3, 1492.)

1. THE Spanish noon is a blaze of azure fire,
and the dusty pilgrims crawl like an endless ser-
pent along treeless plains and bleached high-
roads, through rock-split ravines and castellated,
cathedral-shadowed towns.

2. The hoary patriarch, wrinkled as an al-
mond shell, bows painfully upon his staff. The
beautiful young mother, ivory-pale, well-nigh
swoons beneath her burden ; in her large enfold-
ing arms nestles her sleeping babe, round her
knees flock her little ones with bruised and bleed-
ing feet. " Mother, shall we soon be there ? "

3. The youth with Christ-like countenance
speaks comfortably to father and brother, to

maiden and wife. In his breast, his own heart is broken.

4. The halt, the blind, are amid the train. Sturdy pack-horses laboriously drag the tented wagons wherein lie the sick athirst with fever.

5. The panting mules are urged forward with spur and goad; stuffed are the heavy saddle-bags with the wreckage of ruined homes.

6. Hark to the tinkling silver bells that adorn the tenderly-carried silken scrolls.

7. In the fierce noon-glare a lad bears a kindled lamp; behind its net-work of bronze the airs of heaven breathe not upon its faint purple star.

8. Noble and abject, learned and simple, illustrious and obscure, plod side by side, all brothers now, all merged in one routed army of misfortune.

9. Woe to the straggler who falls by the wayside! no friend shall close his eyes.

10. They leave behind, the grape, the olive, and the fig; the vines they planted, the corn they sowed, the garden-cities of Andalusia and Aragon, Estremadura and La Mancha, of Granada and Castile; the altar, the hearth, and the grave of their fathers.

11. The townsman spits at their garments, the shepherd quits his flock, the peasant his plow, to pelt with curses and stones; the villager sets on their trail his yelping cur.

12. Oh the weary march, oh the uptorn roots of home, oh the blankness of the receding goal!

13. Listen to their lamentation : *They that ate dainty food are desolate in the streets ; they that were reared in scarlet embrace dunghills. They flee away and wander about. Men say among the nations, they shall no more sojourn there ; our end is near, our days are full, our doom is come.*

14. Whither shall they turn? for the West hath cast them out, and the East refuseth to receive.

15. O bird of the air, whisper to the despairing exiles, that to-day, to-day, from the many-masted, gayly-bannered port of Palos, sails the world-unveiling Genoese, to unlock the golden gates of sunset and bequeath a Continent to Freedom!

II. TREASURES.

1. THROUGH cycles of darkness the diamond sleeps in its coal-black prison.

2. Purely incrusted in its scaly casket, the breath - tarnished pearl slumbers in mud and ooze.

3. Buried in the bowels of earth, rugged and obscure, lies the ingot of gold.

4. Long hast thou been buried, O Israel, in the bowels of earth ; long hast thou slumbered beneath the overwhelming waves ; long hast thou slept in the rayless house of darkness,

5. Rejoice and sing, for only thus couldst thou rightly guard the golden knowledge, Truth, the delicate pearl and the adamantine jewel of the Law.

III. THE SOWER.

1. OVER a boundless plain went a man, carrying seed.

2. His face was blackened by sun and rugged from tempest, scarred and distorted by pain. Naked to the loins, his back was ridged with furrows, his breast was plowed with stripes.

3. From his hand dropped the fecund seed.

4. And behold, instantly started from the prepared soil a blade, a sheaf, a springing trunk, a myriad-branching, cloud-aspiring tree. Its arms touched the ends of the horizon, the heavens were darkened with its shadow.

5. It bare blossoms of gold and blossoms of blood, fruitage of health and fruitage of poison; birds sang amid its foliage, and a serpent was coiled about its stem.

6. Under its branches a divinely beautiful man, crowned with thorns, was nailed to a cross.

7. And the tree put forth treacherous boughs to strangle the Sower; his flesh was bruised and torn, but cunningly he disentangled the murderous knot and passed to the eastward.

8. Again there dropped from his hand the fecund seed.

9. And behold, instantly started from the pre-pared soil a blade, a sheaf, a springing trunk, a myriad-branching, cloud-aspiring tree. Cres-cent shaped like little emerald moons were the leaves; it bare blossoms of silver and blossoms of blood, fruitage of health and fruitage of poi-son; birds sang amid its foilage and a serpent was coiled about its stem.

10. Under its branches a turbaned mighty-limbed Prophet brandished a drawn sword.

11. And behold, this tree likewise puts forth perfidious arms to strangle the Sower; but cun-ningly he disentangles the murderous knot and passes on.

12. Lo, his hands are not empty of grain, the strength of his arm is not spent.

13. What germ hast thou saved for the future, O miraculous Husbandman? Tell me, thou Planter of Christhood and Islam; tell me, thou seed-bearing Israel!

IV. THE TEST.

1. DAYLONG I brooded upon the Passion of Israel.

2. I saw him bound to the wheel, nailed to the cross, cut off by the sword, burned at the stake, tossed into the seas.

3. And always the patient, resolute, martyr face arose in silent rebuke and defiance.

4. A Prophet with four eyes; wide gazed the

orbs of the spirit above the sleeping eyelids of the senses.

5. A Poet, who plucked from his bosom the quivering heart and fashioned it into a lyre.

6. A placid-browed Sage, uplifted from earth in celestial meditation.

7. These I saw, with princes and people in their train ; the monumental dead and the stand-ard-bearers of the future.

8. And suddenly I heard a burst of mocking laughter, and turning, I beheld the shuffling gait, the ignominious features, the sordid mask of the son of the Ghetto.

V. CURRENTS.

1. VAST oceanic movements, the flux and re-flux of immeasurable tides, oversweep our conti-nent.

2. From the far Caucasian steppes, from the squalid Ghettos of Europe,

3. From Odessa and Bucharest, from Kief, and Ekaterinoslav,

4. Hark to the cry of the exiles of Babylon, the voice of Rachel mourning for her children, of Israel lamenting for Zion.

5. And lo, like a turbid stream, the long-pent flood bursts the dykes of oppression and rushes hitherward.

6. Unto her ample breast, the generous mother of nations welcomes them.

7. The herdsman of Canaan and the seed of Jerusalem's royal shepherd renew their youth amid the pastoral plains of Texas and the golden valleys of the Sierras.

VI. THE PROPHET.

1. MOSES BEN MAIMON lifting his perpetual lamp over the path of the perplexed;

2. Hallevi, the honey-tongued poet, wakening amid the silent ruins of Zion the sleeping lyre of David;

3. Moses, the wise son of Mendel, who made the Ghetto illustrious;

4. Abarbanel, the counselor of kings; Alcharisi, the exquisite singer; Ibn Ezra, the perfect old man; Gabirol, the tragic seer;

5. Heine, the enchanted magician, the heart-broken jester;

6. Yea, and the century-crowned patriarch whose bounty engirdles the globe; —

7. These need no wreath and no trumpet; like perennial asphodel blossoms, their fame, their glory resounds like the brazen-throated cornet.

8. But thou — hast thou faith in the fortune of Israel? Wouldst thou lighten the anguish of Jacob?

9. Then shalt thou take the hand of yonder caftaned wretch with flowing curls and gold-pierced ears;

10. Who crawls blinking forth from the loathsome recesses of the Jewry ;

11. Nerveless his fingers, puny his frame; haunted by the bat-like phantoms of superstition is his brain.

12. Thou shalt say to the bigot, " My Brother," and to the creature of darkness, " My Friend."

13. And thy heart shall spend itself in fountains of love upon the ignorant, the coarse, and the abject.

14. Then in the obscurity thou shalt hear a rush of wings, thine eyes shall be bitten with pungent smoke.

15. And close against thy quivering lips shall be pressed the live coal wherewith the Seraphim brand the Prophets.

VII. CHRYSALIS.

1. Long, long has the Orient-Jew spun around his helplessness the cunningly enmeshed web of Talmud and Kabbala.

2. Imprisoned in dark corners of misery and oppression, closely he drew about him the dustgray filaments, soft as silk and stubborn as steel, until he lay death-stiffened in mummied seclusion.

3. And the world has named him an ugly worm, shunning the blessed daylight.

4. But when the emancipating springtide

breathes wholesome, quickening airs, when the Sun of Love shines out with cordial fires, lo, the Soul of Israel bursts her cobweb sheath, and flies forth attired in the winged beauty of immortality.

TO CARMEN SYLVA.

OH, that the golden lyre divine
Whence David smote flame-tones were mine!
Oh, that the silent harp which hung
        Untuned, unstrung,
Upon the willows by the river,
Would throb beneath my touch and quiver
With the old song-enchanted spell
        Of Israel!

Oh, that the large prophetic Voice
Would make my reed-piped throat its choice!
All ears should prick, all hearts should spring,
        To hear me sing
The burden of the isles, the word
Assyria knew, Damascus heard,
When, like the wind, while cedars shake,
        Isaiah spake.

For I would frame a song to-day
Winged like a bird to cleave its way
O'er land and sea that spread between,
        To where a Queen

Sits with a triple coronet.
Genius and Sorrow both have set
Their diadems above the gold —
       A Queen three-fold!

To her the forest lent its lyre,
Hers are the sylvan dews, the fire
Of Orient suns, the mist-wreathed gleams
       Of mountain streams.
She, the imperial Rhine's own child,
Takes to her heart the wood-nymph wild,
The gypsy Pelech, and the wide,
       White Danube's tide.

She who beside an infant's bier
Long since resigned all hope to hear
The sacred name of "Mother" bless
       Her childlessness,
Now from a people's sole acclaim
Receives the heart-vibrating name,
And "Mother, Mother, Mother!" fills
       The echoing hills.

Yet who is he who pines apart,
Estranged from that maternal heart,
Ungraced, unfriended, and forlorn,
       The butt of scorn?
An alien in his land of birth,
An outcast from his brethren's earth,
Albeit with theirs his blood mixed well
       When Plevna fell?

When all Roumania's chains were riven,
When unto all his sons was given
The hero's glorious reward,
   Reaped by the sword, —
Wherefore was this poor thrall, whose chains
Hung heaviest, within whose veins
The oldest blood of freedom streamed,
   Still unredeemed?

O Mother, Poet, Queen in one!
Pity and save — he is thy son.
For poet David's sake, the king
   Of all who sing;
For thine own people's sake who share
His law, his truth, his praise, his prayer;
For his sake who was sacrificed —
   His brother — Christ!

THE DANCE TO DEATH;

A HISTORICAL TRAGEDY IN FIVE ACTS.

This play is dedicated, in profound veneration and respect, to the memory of George Eliot, the illustrious writer, who did most among the artists of our day towards elevating and ennobling the spirit of Jewish nationality.

THE PERSONS.

FREDERICK THE GRAVE, *Landgrave of Thuringia and Margrave of Meissen, Protector and Patron of the Free City of Nordhausen.*

PRINCE WILLIAM OF MEISSEN, *his son.*

SÜSSKIND VON ORB, *a Jew.*

HENRY SCHNETZEN, *Governor of Salza.*

HENRY NORDMANN OF NORDMANNSTEIN, *Knight of Treffurt.*

REINHARD PEPPERCORN, *Prior of Wartburg Monastery.*

RABBI JACOB.

DIETRICH VON TETTENBORN, *President of the Council.*

REUBEN VON ORB, *a boy, Süsskind's son.*

BARUCH,
NAPHTALI, } *Jews.*

RABBI CRESSELIN.

LAY-BROTHER.

PAGE.

PUBLIC SCRIVENER.

PRINCESS MATHILDIS, *wife to Frederick.*

LIEBHAID VON ORB.

CLAIRE CRESSELIN.

Jews, Jewesses, Burghers, Senators, Citizens, Citizen's Wife and Boy, Flagellants, Servants, Guardsmen.

Scene — Partly in Nordhausen, partly in Eisenach. Time, May, 4th, 5th, 6th, 1349.

ACT I. — *In Nordhausen.*

SCENE I.

A street in the Judengasse, outside the Synagogue. During this Scene Jews and Jewesses, singly and in groups, with prayer-books in their hands, pass across the stage, and go into the Synagogue. Among them, enter BARUCH *and* NAPHTALI.

NAPHTALI.

Hast seen him yet?

BARUCH.

     Nay ; Rabbi Jacob's door
Swung to behind him, just as I puffed up
O'erblown with haste. See how our years weigh,
   cousin.
Who 'd judge me with this paunch a temperate
   man,
A man of modest means, a man withal
Scarce overpast his prime? Well, God be
   praised,
If age bring no worse burden! Who is this
   stranger?
Simon the Leech tells me he claims to bear
Some special message from the Lord — no
   doubt
To-morrow, fresh from rest, he 'll publish it
Within the Synagogue.

NAPHTALI.

              To-morrow, man?
He will not hear of rest — he comes anon —
Shall we within?

BARUCH.

            Rather let's wait,
And scrutinize him as he mounts the street.
Since you denote him so remarkable,
You've whetted my desire.

NAPHTALI.

              A blind, old man,
Mayhap is all you'll find him — spent with travel,
His raiment fouled with dust, his sandaled feet
Road-bruised by stone and bramble. But his
      face! —
Majestic with long fall of cloud-white beard,
And hoary wreath of hair — oh, it is one
Already kissed by angels.

BARUCH.

              Look, there limps
Little Manasseh, bloated as his purse,
And wrinkled as a frost-pinched fruit. I hear
His last loan to the Syndic will result
In quadrupling his wealth. Good Lord! what
      luck
Blesses some folk, while good men stint and
      sweat

And scrape, to merely fill the household larder.
What said you of this pilgrim, Naphtali?
These inequalities of fortune rub
My sense of justice so against the grain,
I lose my very name.   Whence does he come?
Is he alone?

NAPHTALI.

He comes from Chinon, France.
Rabbi Cresselin he calls himself — alone
Save for his daughter who has led him hither.
A beautiful, pale girl with round black eyes.

BARUCH.

Bring they fresh tidings of the pestilence?

NAPHTALI.

I know not — but I learn from other source
It has burst forth at Erfurt.

BARUCH.

God have mercy!
Have many of our tribe been stricken?

NAPHTALI.

No.
They cleanse their homes and keep their bodies
        sweet,
Nor cease from prayer — and so does Jacob's
        God

Protect His chosen, still.   Yet even His favor
Our enemies would twist into a curse.
Beholding the destroying angel smite
The foul idolater and leave unscathed
The gates of Israel — the old cry they raise —
We have begotten the Black Death — *we* poison
The well-springs of the towns.

BARUCH.

                         God pity us!
But truly are we blessed in Nordhausen.
Such terrors seem remote as Egypt's plagues.
I warrant you our Landgrave dare not harry
Such creditors as we.   See, here comes one,
The greatest and most liberal of them all —
Süsskind von Orb.

SÜSSKIND VON ORB, LIEBHAID, *and* REUBEN *enter, all
    pass across the stage, and disappear within the Syna-
    gogue.*

                         I'd barter my whole fortune,
And yours to boot, that's thrice the bulk of
    mine,
For half the bonds he holds in Frederick's name.
The richest merchant in Thuringia, he —
The poise of his head would tell it, knew we
    not.
How has his daughter leaped to womanhood!
I mind when she came toddling by his hand,
But yesterday — a flax-haired child — to-day
Her brow is level with his pompous chin.

NAPHTALI.

How fair she is! Her hair has kept its gold
Untarnished still. I trace not either parent
In her face, clean cut as a gem.

BARUCH.

Her mother
Was far-off kin to me, and I might pass,
I 'm told, unguessed in Christian garb. I know
A pretty secret of that scornful face.
It lures high game to Nordhausen.

NAPHTALI.

Baruch,
I marvel at your prompt credulity.
The Prince of Meissen and Liebhaid von Orb!
A jest for gossips and — Look, look, he comes!

BARUCH.

Who 's that, the Prince?

NAPHTALI.

Nay, dullard, the old man,
The Rabbi of Chinon. Ah! his stout staff,
And that brave creature's strong young hand
        suffice
Scarcely to keep erect his tottering frame.
Emaciate-lipped, with cavernous black eyes
Whose inward visions do eclipse the day,

Seems he not one re-risen from the grave
To yield the secret ?

Enter RABBI JACOB, *and* RABBI CRESSELIN *led by*
    CLAIRE. *They walk across the stage, and disappear in*
    the Synagogue.

BARUCH (*exaltedly*).

Blessed art thou, O Lord,
King of the Universe, who teachest wisdom
To those who fear thee ! [1]

NAPHTALI.

Haste we in.   The star
Of Sabbath dawns.

BARUCH.

My flesh is still a-creep
From the strange gaze of those wide-rolling
    orbs.
Didst note, man, how they fixed me ?   His lean
    cheeks,
As wan as wax, were bloodless ; how his arms
Stretched far beyond the flowing sleeve and
    showed
Gaunt, palsied wrists, and hands blue-tipped with
    death !
Well, I have seen a sage of Israel.

[*They enter the Synagogue.   Scene closes.*

[1] These words are the customary formula of Jewish
prayer on seeing a wise man of Israel.

SCENE II.

The Synagogue crowded with worshippers. Among the women in the Gallery are discovered LIEBHAID VON ORB *and* CLAIRE CRESSELIN. *Below, among the men,* SÜSS- KIND VON ORB *and* REUBEN. *At the Reader's Desk,* RABBI JACOB. *Fronting the audience under the Ark of the Covenant, stands a high desk, behind which is seen the white head of an old man bowed in prayer.* BARUCH *and* NAPHTALI *enter and take their seats.*

BARUCH.

Think you he speaks before the service ?

NAPHTALI.

Yea.

Lo, phantom-like the towering patriarch !
   [RABBI CRESSELIN *slowly rises beneath the Ark.*

RABBI CRESSELIN.

Woe unto Israel ! woe unto all
Abiding 'mid strange peoples ! Ye shall be
Cut off from that land where ye made your
   home.
I, Cresselin of Chinon, have traveled far,
Thence where my fathers dwelt, to warn my
   race,
For whom the fire and stake have been prepared.
Our brethren of Verdun, all over France,
Are burned alive beneath the *Goyim's* torch.
What terrors have I witnessed, ere my sight
Was mercifully quenched !   In Gascony,

In Savoy, Piedmont, round the garden shores
Of tranquil Leman, down the beautiful Rhine,
At Lindau, Costnitz, Schaffhausen, St. Gallen,
Everywhere torture, smoking Synagogues,
Carnage, and burning flesh. The lights shine
    out
Of Jewish virtue, Jewish truth, to star
The sanguine field with an immortal blazon.
The venerable Mar-Isaac in Cologne,
Sat in his house at prayer, nor lifted lid
From off the sacred text, while all around
The fanatics ran riot ; him they seized,
Haled through the streets, with prod of stick and
    spike
Fretted his wrinkled flesh, plucked his white
    beard,
Dragged him with gibes into their Church, and
    held
A Crucifix before him.   " Know thy Lord ! "
He spat thereon ; he was pulled limb from limb.
I saw — God, that I might forget ! — a man
Leap in the Loire, with his fair, stalwart son,
A-bloom with youth, and midst the stream un-
    sheathe
A poniard, sheathing it in his boy's heart,
While he pronounced the blessing for the dead.
"Amen ! " the lad responded as he sank,
And the white water darkened as with wine.
I saw — but no ! You are glutted, and my
    tongue,

Blistered, refuseth to narrate more woe.
I have known much sorrow.   When it pleased
     the Lord
To afflict us with the horde of *Pastoureaux*,
The rabble of armed herdsmen, peasants, slaves,
Men-beasts of burden — coarse as the earth they
     tilled,
Who like an inundation deluged France
To drown our race — my heart held firm, my
     faith
Shook not upon her rock until I saw,
Smit by God's beam, the big black cloud dis-
     solve.
Then followed with their scythes, spades, clubs,
     and banners
Flaunting the Cross, the hosts of Armleder,
From whose fierce wounds we scarce are healed
     to-day.
Yet do I say the cup of bitterness
That Israel has drained is but a draught
Of cordial, to the cup that is prepared.
The Black Death and the Brothers of the Cross,
These are our foes — and these are everywhere.
I who am blind see ruin in their wake ;
Ye who have eyes and limbs, arise and flee !
To-morrow the Flagellants will be here.
God's angel visited my sleep and spake :
" Thy Jewish kin in the Thuringian town
Of Nordhausen shall be swept off from earth,
Their elders and their babes — consumed with
     fire.

Go, summon Israel to flight — take this
As sign that I, who call thee, am the Lord,
Thine eyes shalt be struck blind till thou hast
    spoken."
Then darkness fell upon my mortal sense,
But light broke o'er my soul, and all was clear,
And I have journeyed hither with my child
O'er mount and river, till I have announced
The message of the Everlasting God.

                    [*Sensation in the Synagogue.*

RABBI JACOB.

Father, have mercy! when wilt thou have done
With rod and scourge?   Beneath thy children's
    feet
Earth splits, fire springs. No rest, no rest! no rest,

A VOICE.

Look to the women! Mariamne swoons!

ANOTHER VOICE.

Woe unto us who sinned!

ANOTHER VOICE.

                    We 're all dead men.
Fly, fly ere dawn as our forefathers fled
From out the land of Egypt.

BARUCH.

                    Are ye mad?
Shall we desert snug homes? forego the sum

Scraped through laborious years to smooth life's
　　slope,
And die like dogs unkenneled and untombed,
At bidding of a sorrow-crazed old man?

A VOICE.

He flouts the Lord's anointed! Cast him forth!

SÜSSKIND VON ORB.

Peace, brethren, peace! If I have ever served
Israel with purse, arm, brain, or heart — now
　　hear me!
May God instruct my speech! This wise old
　　man,
Whose brow flames with the majesty of truth,
May be part-blinded through excess of light,
As one who eyes too long the naked sun,
Setting in rayless glory, turns and finds
Outlines confused, familiar colors changed,
All objects branded with one blood-bright spot.
Nor chafe at Baruch's homely sense; truth floats
Midway between the stars and the abyss.
We, by God's grace, have found a special nest
I' the dangerous rock, screened against wind
　　and hawk;
Free burghers of a free town, blessed moreover
With the peculiar favor of the Prince,
Frederick the Grave, our patron and protector.
What shall we fear? Rather, where shall we
　　seek

Secure asylum, if here be not one ?
Fly ?   Our forefathers had the wilderness,
The sea their gateway, and the fire-cored cloud
Their divine guide. Us, hedged by ambushed
    foes,
No frank, free, kindly desert shall receive.
Death crouches on all sides, prepared to leap
Tiger-like on our throats, when first we step
From this safe covert.   Everywhere the Plague !
As nigh as Erfurt it has crawled — the towns
Reek with miasma, the rank fields of spring,
Rain-saturated, are one beautiful — lie,
Smiling profuse life, and secreting death.
Strange how, unbidden, a trivial memory
Thrusts itself on my mind in this grave hour.
I saw a large white bull urged through the town
To slaughter, by a stripling with a goad,
Whom but one sure stamp of that solid heel,
One toss of those mooned horns, one battering
    blow
Of that square marble forehead, would have
    crushed,
As we might crush a worm, yet on he trudged,
Patient, in powerful health to death.   At once,
As though o' the sudden stung, he roared aloud,
Beat with fierce hoofs the air, shook desperately
His formidable head, and heifer-swift,
Raced through scared, screaming streets.   Well,
    and the end ?
He was the promptlier bound and killed and
    quartered.

The world belongs to man; dreams the poor
    brute
Some nook has been apportioned for brute life?
Where shall a man escape men's cruelty?
Where shall God's servant cower from his
    doom?
Let us bide, brethren — we are in His hand.

RABBI CRESSELIN (*uttering a piercing shriek*).

                        Ah!

Woe unto Israel!   Lo, I see again,
As the Ineffable foretold.   I see
A flood of fire that streams towards the town.
Look, the destroying Angel with the sword,
Wherefrom the drops of gall are raining down,
Broad-winged, comes flying towards you.   Now
    he draws
His lightning-glittering blade!   With the keen
    edge
He smiteth Israel — ah!

    [*He falls back dead.   Confusion in the Synagogue.*

CLAIRE (*from the gallery*).

                    Father!   My father!
Let me go down to him!

LIEBHAID.

                    Sweet girl, be patient.
This is the House of God, and He hath entered.
Bow we and pray.

[*Meanwhile, some of the men surround and raise from the ground the body of* RABBI CRESSELIN. *Several voices speaking at once.*

1ST VOICE.

He's doomed.

2D VOICE.

Dead! Dead!

3D VOICE.

A judgment!

4TH VOICE.

Make way there! Air! Carry him forth! He's warm!

3D VOICE.

Nay, his heart's stopped — his breath has ceased — quite dead.

5TH VOICE.

Didst mark a diamond lance flash from the roof,
And strike him 'twixt the eyes?

1ST VOICE.

Our days are numbered.
This is the token.

RABBI JACOB.
                    Lift the corpse and pray.
Shall we neglect God's due observances,
While He is manifest in miracle?
I saw a blaze seven times more bright than fire,
Crest, halo-wise, the patriarch's white head.
The dazzle stung my burning lids — they closed,
One instant — when they oped, the great blank
        cloud
Had settled on his countenance forever.
[1] Departed brother, mayest thou find the gates
Of heaven open, see the city of peace,
And meet the ministering angels, glad,
Hastening towards thee! May the High Priest
        stand
To greet and bless thee! Go thou to the end!
Repose in peace and rise again to life.
No more thy sun sets, neither wanes thy moon.
The Lord shall be thy everlasting light,
Thy days of mourning shall be at an end.
For you, my flock, fear nothing; it is writ
As one his mother comforteth, so I
Will comfort you and in Jerusalem
Ye shall be comforted.   [*Scene closes.*

  [1] From this point to the end of the scene is a literal
translation of the Hebrew burial service.

SCENE III.

Evening. A crooked byway in the Judengasse. Enter
PRINCE WILLIAM.

PRINCE WILLIAM.

Cursed be these twisted lanes! I have missed
  the clue
Of the close labyrinth. Nowhere in sight,
Just when I lack it, a stray gaberdine
To pick me up my thread. Yet when I haste
Through these blind streets, unwishful to be spied,
Some dozen hawk-eyes peering o'er crook'd
  beaks
Leer recognition, and obsequious caps
Do kiss the stones to greet my princeship. Bah!
Strange, 'midst such refuse sleeps so white a
  pearl.
At last, here shuffles one.

Enter a Jew.
       Give you good even!
Sir, can you help me to the nighest way
Unto the merchant's house, Süsskind von Orb?

JEW.

Whence come you knowing not the high brick
  wall,
Without, blank as my palm, o' the inner side,
Muring a palace? But — do you wish him well?
He is my friend — we must be wary, wary,

We all have warning — Oh, the terror of it !
I have not yet my wits !

PRINCE WILLIAM.

                              I am his friend.
Is he in peril?   What's the matter, man?

JEW.

Peril?   His peril is no worse than mine,
But the rich win compassion.   God is just,
And every man of us is doomed.   Alack !
He said it — oh those wild, white eyes !

PRINCE WILLIAM.

                                        I pray you,
Tell me the way to Süsskind's home.

JEW.

                                        Sweet master,
You look the perfect knight, what can you crave
Of us starved, wretched Jews?   Leave us in
        peace.
The Judengasse gates will shut anon,
Nor ope till morn again for Jew or Gentile.

PRINCE WILLIAM.

Here's gold.   I am the Prince of Meissen —
        speak !

JEW.

Oh pardon !   Let me kiss your mantle's edge.
This way, great sir, I lead you there myself,

If you deign follow one so poor, so humble.
You must show mercy in the name of God,
For verily are we afflicted.   Come.
Hard by is Süsskind's dwelling — as we walk
By your good leave I 'll tell what I have seen.

[Exeunt.

SCENE IV.

A luxuriously-furnished apartment in Süsskind von
Orb's *house.   Upon a richly-spread supper-table stands
the seven-branched silver candlestick of the Sabbath eve.
At the table are seated* Süsskind von Orb, Liebhaid,
and Reuben.

SÜSSKIND.

Drink, children, drink! and lift your hearts to
    Him
Who gives us the vine's fruit.   [*They drink.*
               How clear it glows;
Like gold within the golden bowl, like fire
Along our veins, after the work-day week
Rekindling Sabbath-fervor, Sabbath-strength.
Verily God prepares for me a table
In presence of mine enemies!   He anoints
My head with oil, my cup is overflowing.
Praise we His name!   Hast thou, my daughter,
    served
The needs o' the poor, suddenly-orphaned child?
Naught must she lack beneath my roof.

LIEBHAID.

Yea, father.

She prays and weeps within : she had no heart
For Sabbath meal, but charged me with her
    thanks —

SÜSSKIND.

Thou shalt be mother and sister in one to her.
Speak to her comfortably.

REUBEN.

She has begged
A grace of me I happily can grant.
After our evening-prayer, to lead her back
Unto the Synagogue, where sleeps her father,
A light at head and foot, o'erwatched by
    strangers ;
She would hold vigil.

SÜSSKIND.

'T is a pious wish,
Not to be crossed, befitting Israel's daughter.
Go, Reuben ; heavily the moments hang,
While her heart yearns to break beside his
    corpse.
Receive my blessing.

> [*He places his hands upon his son's head in benediction. Exit Reuben.*

Henceforth her home is here.
In the event to-night, God's finger points

Visibly out of heaven.   A thick cloud
Befogs the future.   But just here is light.

Enter a servant ushering in PRINCE WILLIAM.

SERVANT.

His highness Prince of Meissen.   [*Exit.*

SÜSSKIND.

Welcome, Prince!
God bless thy going forth and coming in!
Sit at our table and accept the cup
Of welcome which my daughter fills.

[LIEBHAID *offers him wine.*

PRINCE WILLIAM (*drinking*).

To thee!
[*All take their seats at the table.*

I heard disquieting news as I came hither.
The apparition in the Synagogue,
The miracle of the message and the death.
Süsskind von Orb, what think'st thou of these
        things?

SÜSSKIND.

I think, sir, we are in the hand of God,
I trust the Prince — your father and my friend.

PRINCE WILLIAM.

Trust no man! flee!   I have not come to-night
To little purpose.   Your arch enemy,
The Governor of Salza, Henry Schnetzen,
Has won my father's ear.   Since yester eve

He stops at Eisenach, begging of the Prince
The Jews' destruction.

SÜSSKIND (*calmly*).

                        Schnetzen is my foe,
I know it, but I know a talisman,
Which at a word transmutes his hate to love.
Liebhaid, my child, look cheerly.   What is this?
Harm dare not touch thee; the oppressor's curse,
Melts into blessing at thy sight.

LIEBHAID.

                        Not fear
Plucks at my heart-strings, father, though the air
Thickens with portents; 't is the thought of
        flight,
But no — I follow thee.

PRINCE WILLIAM.

                        Thou shalt not miss
The value of a hair from thy home treasures.
All that thou lovest, Liebhaid, goes with thee.
Knowest thou, Süsskind, Schnetzen's cause of
        hate?

SÜSSKIND.

'T is rooted in an ancient error, born
During his feud with Landgrave Fritz the Bitten,
Your Highness' grandsire — ten years — twenty
        —back.

Misled to think I had betrayed his castle,
Who knew the secret tunnel to its courts,
He has nursed a baseless grudge, whereat I smile,
Sure to disarm him by the simple truth.
God grant me strength to utter it.

PRINCE WILLIAM.

                                You fancy
The rancor of a bad heart slow distilled
Through venomed years, so at a breath, dissolves.
O good old man, i' the world, not of the world!
Belike, himself forgets the doubtful core
Of this still-curdling, petrifying ooze.
Truth? why truth glances from the callous mass,
A spear against a rock.   He hugs his hate,
His bed-fellow, his daily, life-long comrade;
Think you he has slept, ate, drank with it this
         while,
Now to forego revenge on such slight cause
As the revealed truth?

SÜSSKIND.

              You mistake my thought,
Great-hearted Prince, and justly — for I speak
In riddles, till God's time to make all clear.
When His day dawns, the blind shall see.

PRINCE WILLIAM.

                                Forgive me,
If I, in wit and virtue your disciple,

Seem to instruct my master.   Accident
Lifts me where I survey a broader field
Than wise men stationed lower.   I spy peril,
Fierce flame invisible from the lesser peaks.
God's time is now.   Delayed truth leaves a lie
Triumphant.   If you harbor any secret,
Potent to force an ear that 's locked to mercy,
In God's name, now disbosom it.

SÜSSKIND.

                              Kind Heaven!
Would that my people's safety were assured
So is my child's!   Where shall we turn ?   Where
     flee?
For all around us the Black Angel broods.
We step into the open jaws of death
If we go hence.

PRINCE WILLIAM.

                    Better to fall beneath
The hand of God, than be cut off by man.

SÜSSKIND.

We are trapped, the springe is set.   Not igno-
     rantly
I offered counsel in the Synagogue,
Quelled panic with authoritative calm,
But knowing, having weighed the opposing risks.
Our friends in Strasburg have been overmastered,
The imperial voice is drowned, the papal arm

Drops paralyzed — both, lifted for the truth;
We can but front with brave eyes, brow erect,
As is our wont, the fullness of our doom.

PRINCE WILLIAM.

Then Meissen's sword champions your desperate
cause.
I take my stand here where my heart is fixed.
I love your daughter — if her love consent,
I pray you, give me her to wife.

LIEBHAID.

Ah!

SÜSSKIND.

Prince,
Let not this Saxon skin, this hair's gold fleece,
These Rhine-blue eyes mislead thee — she is
alien.
To the heart's core a Jewess — prop of my
house,
Soul of my soul — and I? a despised Jew.

PRINCE WILLIAM.

Thy propped house crumbles; let my arm sus-
tain
Its tottering base — thy light is on the wane,
Let me relume it. Give thy star to me,
Or ever pitch-black night engulf us all —
Lend me your voice, Liebhaid, entreat for me.
Shall this prayer be your first that he denies?

LIEBHAID.

Father, my heart's desire is one with his.

SÜSSKIND.

Is this the will of God ? Amen ! My children,
Be patient with me, I am full of trouble.
For you, heroic Prince, could aught enhance
Your love's incomparable nobility,
'T were the foreboding horror of this hour,
Wherein you dare flash forth its lightning-sword.
You reckon not, in the hot, splendid moment
Of great resolve, the cold insidious breath
Wherewith the outer world shall blast and
        freeze —
But hark ! I own a mystic amulet,
Which you delivering to your gracious father,
Shall calm his rage withal, and change his scorn
Of the Jew's daughter into pure affection.
I will go fetch it — though I drain my heart
Of its red blood, to yield this sacrifice.

                              [*Exit* SÜSSKIND.

PRINCE WILLIAM.

Have you no smile to welcome love with, Lieb-
        haid ?
Why should you tremble ?

LIEBHAID.

                              Prince, I am afraid !
Afraid of my own heart, my unfathomed joy,

A blasphemy against my father's grief,
My people's agony.   I dare be happy —
So happy ! in the instant's lull betwixt
The dazzle and the crash of doom.

PRINCE WILLIAM.

You read
The omen falsely ; rather is your joy
The thrilling harbinger of general dawn.
Did you not tell me scarce a month agone,
When I chanced in on you at feast and prayer,
The holy time's bright legend ? of the queen,
Strong, beautiful, resolute, who denied her race
To save her race, who cast upon the die
Of her divine and simple loveliness,
Her life, her soul, — and so redeemed her tribe.
You are my Esther — but I, no second tyrant,
Worship whom you adore, love whom you love !

LIEBHAID.

If I must die with morn, I thank my God,
And thee, my king, that I have lived this night.

Enter SÜSSKIND, *carrying a jewelled casket.*

SÜSSKIND.

Here is the chest, sealed with my signet-ring,
A mystery and a treasure lies within,
Whose worth is faintly symboled by these gems,
Starring the case.   Deliver it unopened,

Unto the Landgrave.   Now, sweet Prince, good
    night.
Else will the Judengasse gates be closed.

PRINCE WILLIAM.

Thanks, father, thanks.   Liebhaid, my bride,
    good-night.
> [*He kisses her brow.* SÜSSKIND *places his hands on
> the heads of* LIEBHAID *and* PRINCE WILLIAM.

SÜSSKIND.

Blessed, O Lord, art thou, who bringest joy
To bride and bridegroom.   Let us thank the
    Lord.   [*Curtain falls.*

ACT II. — *At Eisenach.*

SCENE I.

A Room in the LANDGRAVE'S *Palace.*   FREDERICK THE
GRAVE *and* HENRY SCHNETZEN.

LANDGRAVE.

Who tells thee of my son's love for the Jewess ?

SCHNETZEN.

Who tells me ?   Ask the Judengasse walls,
The garrulous stones publish Prince William's
    visits
To his fair mistress.

LANDGRAVE.

　　　　　Mistress?　Ah, such sins
The Provost of St. George's will remit
For half a pound of coppers.

SCHNETZEN.

　　　　　　　Think it not!
No light amour this, leaving shield unflecked ;
He wooes the Jewish damsel as a knight
The lady of his heart.

LANDGRAVE.

　　　　　　Impossible!

SCHNETZEN.

Things more impossible have chanced.　Re-
　　member
Count Gleichen, doubly wived, who pined in
　　Egypt,
There wed the Pasha's daughter Malachsala,
Nor blushed to bring his heathen paramour
Home to his noble wife Angelica,
Countess of Orlamund.　Yea, and the Pope
Sanctioned the filthy sin.

LANDGRAVE.

　　　　　　Himself shall say it.
Ho, Gunther!　(*Enter a Lackey.*)　Bid the Prince
　　of Meissen here.

　　　[*Exit Lackey.　The* LANDGRAVE *paces the stage in
　　agitation.*

Enter PRINCE WILLIAM.

PRINCE WILLIAM.

Father, you called me?

LANDGRAVE.

                  Ay, when were you last
In Nordhausen?

PRINCE WILLIAM.

          This morning I rode hence.

LANDGRAVE.

Were you at Süsskind's house?

PRINCE WILLIAM.

                  I was, my liege.

LANDGRAVE.

I hear you entertain unseemly love
For the Jew's daughter.

PRINCE WILLIAM.

             Who has told thee this?

SCHNETZEN.

This I have told him.

PRINCE WILLIAM.

          Father, believe him not.
I swear by heaven 't is no unseemly love
Leads me to Süsskind's house.

LANDGRAVE.

                    With what high title
Please you to qualify it?

PRINCE WILLIAM.

                    True, I love
Liebhaid von Orb, but 't is the honest passion
Wherewith a knight leads home his equal wife.

LANDGRAVE.

Great God! and thou wilt brag thy shame!
        Thou speakest
Of wife and Jewess in one breath!   Wilt make
Thy princely name a stench in German nostrils?

PRINCE WILLIAM.

Hold, father, hold!   You know her — yes, a
        Jewess
In her domestic piety, her soul
Large, simple, splendid like a star, her heart
Suffused with Syrian sunshine — but no more —
The aspect of a Princess of Thuringia,
Swan-necked, gold-haired, Madonna-eyed. I love
        her!
If you will quench this passion, take my life!

> [*He falls at his father's feet.* FREDERICK, *in a
> paroxysm of rage, seizes his sword.*

SCHNETZEN.

He is your son!

LANDGRAVE.

Oh that he ne'er were born!
Hola! Halberdiers! Yeomen of the Guard!
Enter Guardsmen.
Bear off this prisoner!   Let him sigh out
His blasphemous folly in the castle tower,
Until his hair be snow, his fingers claws.

[*They seize and bear away* PRINCE WILLIAM.
Well, what 's your counsel?

SCHNETZEN.

Briefly this, my lord.
The Jews of Nordhausen have brewed the
    Prince
A love-elixir — let them perish all!

[*Tumult without.   Singing of Hymns and Ringing
of Church-bells.   The* LANDGRAVE *and* SCHNET-
ZEN *go to the window.*

[1] SONG (*without*).

The cruel pestilence arrives,
Cuts off a myriad human lives.
See the Flagellants' naked skin!
They scourge themselves for grievous sin.
Trembles the earth beneath God's breath,
The Jews shall all be burned to death.

LANDGRAVE.

Look, foreign pilgrims!   What an endless file!

[1] A rhyme of the times.   See Graetz's *History of the
Jews*, page 374, vol. vii.

Naked waist-upward. Blood is trickling down
Their lacerated flesh. What do they carry?

SCHNETZEN.

Their scourges — iron-pointed, leathern thongs,
Mark how they lash themselves — the strict
    Flagellants.
The Brothers of the Cross — hark to their cries!

VOICE FROM BELOW.

Atone, ye mighty! God is wroth! Expel
The enemies of heaven — raze their homes!

> [*Confused cries from below, which gradually die
> away in the distance.*

Woe to God's enemies! Death to the Jews!
They poison all our wells — they bring the
    plague.
Kill them who killed our Lord! Their homes
    shall be
A wilderness — drown them in their own blood!

> [*The* LANDGRAVE *and* SCHNETZEN *withdraw from
> the window.*

SCHNETZEN.

Do not the people ask the same as I?
Is not the people's voice the voice of God?

LANDGRAVE.

I will consider.

SCHNETZEN.

                    Not too long, my liege.
The moment favors.   Later 't were hard to
      show
Due cause to his Imperial Majesty,
For slaughtering the vassals of the Crown.
Two mighty friends are theirs.   His holiness
Clement the Sixth and Kaiser Karl.

LANDGRAVE.

                              'T were rash
Contending with such odds.

SCHNETZEN.

                              Courage, my lord.
These battle singly against death and fate.
Your allies are the sense and heart o' the
      world.
Priests warring for their Christ, nobles for
      gold,
And peoples for the very breath of life
Spoiled by the poison-mixers.   Kaiser Karl
Lifts his lone voice unheard, athwart the roar
Of such a flood; the papal bull is whirled
An unconsidered rag amidst the eddies.

LANDGRAVE.

What credence lend you to the general rumor
Of the river poison?

SCHNETZEN.

Such as mine eyes avouch.
I have seen, yea touched the leathern wallet
    found
On the body of one from whom the truth was
    wrenched
By salutary torture.   He confessed,
Though but a famulus of the master-wizard,
The horrible old Moses of Mayence,
He had flung such pouches in the Rhine, the
    Elbe,
The Oder, Danube — in a hundred brooks,
Until the wholesome air reeked pestilence;
'T was an ell long, filled with a dry, fine dust
Of rusty black and red, deftly compounded
Of powdered flesh of basilisks, spiders, frogs,
And lizards, baked with sacramental dough
In Christian blood.

LANDGRAVE.

Such goblin-tales may curdle
The veins of priest-rid women, fools, and chil-
    dren.
They are not for the ears of sober men.

SCHNETZEN.

Pardon me, Sire.   I am a simple soldier.
My God, my conscience, and my suzerain,
These are my guides — blindfold I follow them.

If your keen royal wit pierce the gross web
Of common superstition — be not wroth
At your poor vassal's loyal ignorance.
Remember, too, Süsskind retains your bonds.
The old fox will not press you; he would bleed
Against the native instinct of the Jew,
Rather his last gold doit and so possess
Your ease of mind, nag, chafe, and toy with it;
Abide his natural death, and other Jews
Less devilish-cunning, franklier Hebrew-viced,
Will claim redemption of your pledge.

LANDGRAVE.

How know you
That Süsskind holds my bonds?

SCHNETZEN.

You think the Jews
Keep such things secret?   Not a Jew but knows
Your debt exact — the sum and date of interest,
And that you visit Süsskind, not for love,
But for his shekels.

LANDGRAVE.

Well, the Jews shall die.
This is the will of God.   Whom shall I send
To bear my message to the council?

SCHNETZEN.

I
Am ever at your 'hest.   To-morrow morn
Sees me in Nordhausen.

LANDGRAVE.

Come two hours hence.
I will deliver you the letter signed.
Make ready for your ride.

SCHNETZEN (*kisses* FREDERICK'S *hand*).

Farewell, my master.
(*Aside.*)   Ah, vengeance cometh late, Süsskind von
    Orb,
But yet it comes!   My wife was burned through
    thee,
Thou and thy children are consumed by me !
[*Exit.*

SCENE II.

A Room in the Wartburg Monastery. PRINCESS MA-
THILDIS *and* PRIOR PEPPERCORN.

PRIOR.

Be comforted, my daughter.   Your lord's wis-
    dom
Goes hand in hand with his known piety
Thus dealing with your son.   To love a Jewess
Is flat contempt of Heaven — to ask in mar-
    riage,
Sheer spiritual suicide.   Let be ;
Justice must take its course.

PRINCESS.

                    Justice is murdered ;
Oh slander not her corpse.   For my son's fault,
A thousand innocents are doomed.   Is that
God's justice ?

PRIOR.

                  Yea, our liege is but his servant.
Did not He purge with fiery hail those twain
Blotches of festering sin, Gomorrah, Sodom?
The Jews are never innocent, — when Christ
Agonized on the Cross, they cried — " His blood
Be on our children's heads and ours ! "   I mark
A dangerous growing evil of these days,
Pity, misnamed — say, criminal indulgence
Of reprobates brow-branded by the Lord.
Shall we excel the Christ in charity ?
Because his law is love, we tutor him
In mercy and reward his murderers ?
Justice is blind and virtue is austere.
If the true passion brimmed our yearning hearts
The vision of the agony would loom
Fixed vividly between the day and us : —
Nailed on the gaunt black Cross the divine form,
Wax - white and dripping blood from ankles,
        wrists,
The sacred ichor that redeems the world,
And crowded in strange shadow of eclipse,
Reviling Jews, wagging their heads accursed,

Sputtering blasphemy —who then would shrink
From holy vengeance? who would offer less
Heroic wrath and filial zeal to God
Than to a murdered father?

PRINCESS.

But my son
Will die with her he loves.

PRIOR.

Better to perish
In time than in eternity. No question
Pends here of individual life; our sight
Must broaden to embrace the scope sublime
Of this trans-earthly theme. The Jew survives
Sword, plague, fire, cataclysm — and must, since
        Christ
Cursed him to live till doomsday, still to be
A scarecrow to the nations. None the less
Are we beholden in Christ's name at whiles,
When maggot-wise Jews breed, infest, infect
Communities of Christians, to wash clean
The Church's vesture, shaking off the filth
That gathers round her skirts. A perilous
        germ!
Know you not, all the wells, the very air
The Jews have poisoned? — Through their arts
        alone
The Black Death scourges Christendom.

PRINCESS.

I know
All heinousness imputed by their foes.
Father, mistake me not : I urge no plea
To shield this hell-spawn, loathed by all who love
The lamb and kiss the Cross. I had not guessed
Such obscure creatures crawled upon my path,
Had not my son — I know not how misled —
Deigned to ennoble with his great regard,
A sparkle midst the dust motes. *She* is sacred.
What is her tribe to me ? Her kith and kin
May rot or roast — the Jews of Nordhausen
May hang, drown, perish like the Jews of
          France,
But she shall live — Liebhaid von Orb, the
          Jewess,
The Prince, my son, elects to love.

PRIOR.

Amen !
Washed in baptismal waters she shall be
Led like the clean-fleeced yeanling to the fold.
Trust me, my daughter — for through me the
          Church
Which is the truth, which is the life, doth speak.
Yet first 't were best essay to cure the Prince
Of his moon-fostered madness, bred, no doubt,
By baneful potions which these cunning knaves
Are skilled to mix.

PRINCESS.

Go visit him, dear father,
Where in the high tower mewed, a wing-clipped
eagle,
His spirit breaks in cage.   You are his master,
He is wont from childhood to hear wisdom fall
From your instructed lips.   Tell him his mother
Rises not from her knees, till he is freed.

PRIOR.

Madam, I go.   Our holy Church has healed
Far deadlier heart-wounds than a love-sick boy's.
Be of good cheer, the Prince shall live to bless
The father's rigor who kept pure of blot
A 'scutcheon more unsullied than the sun.

PRINCESS.

Thanks and farewell.

PRIOR.

Farewell.   God send thee peace !   [*Exeunt.*

SCENE III.

*A mean apartment in one of the Towers of the Landgrave's
Palace.* PRINCE WILLIAM *discovered seated at the
window.*

PRINCE WILLIAM.

The slow sun sets ; with lingering, large embrace
He folds the enchanted hill ; then like a god

Strides into heaven behind the purple peak.
Oh beautiful!   In the clear, rayless air,
I see the chequered vale mapped far below,
The sky-paved streams, the velvet pasture-slopes,
The grim, gray cloister whose deep vesper bell
Blends at this height with tinkling, homebound
      herds!
I see — but oh, how far! — the blessed town
Where Liebhaid dwells.   Oh that I were yon star
That pricks the West's unbroken foil of gold,
Bright as an eye, only to gaze on her!
How keen it sparkles o'er the Venusburg!
When brown night falls and mists begin to live,
Then will the phantom hunting-train emerge,
Hounds straining, black fire - eyeballed, breath-
      less steeds,
Spurred by wild huntsmen, and unhallowed
      nymphs,
And at their head the foam-begotten witch,
Of soul-destroying beauty.   Saints of heaven!
Preserve mine eyes from such unholy sight!
How all unlike the base desire which leads
Misguided men to that infernal cave,
Is the pure passion that exalts my soul
Like a religion!   Yet Christ pardon me,
If this be sin to thee!

> [*He takes his lute, and begins to sing.   Enter with a
> lamp Steward of the Castle, followed by* PRIOR
> PEPPERCORN. *Steward lays down the lamp and
> exit.*

Good even, father!

PRIOR.

Benedicite!
Our bird makes merry his dull bars with song,
Yet would not penitential psalms accord
More fitly with your sin than minstrels' lays?

PRINCE WILLIAM.

I know no blot upon my life's fair record.

PRIOR.

What is it to wanton with a Christ‑cursed
Jewess,
Defy thy father and pollute thy name,
And fling to the ordures thine immortal soul?

PRINCE WILLIAM.

Forbear! thy cowl 's a helmet, thy serge frock
Invulnerable as brass — yet I am human,
Thou, priest, art still a man.

PRIOR.

Pity him, Heaven!
To what a pass their draughts have brought the
mildest,
Noblest of princes! Softly, my son; be ruled
By me, thy spiritual friend and father.
Thou hast been drugged with sense-deranging
potions,
Thy blood set boiling and thy brain askew;

When these thick fumes subside, thou shalt
  awake
To bless the friend who gave thy madness
  bounds.

PRINCE WILLIAM.

Madness! Yea, as the sane world goes, I am
  mad.
What else to help the helpless, to uplift
The low, to adore the good, the beautiful,
To live, battle, suffer, die for truth, for love !
But that is wide of the question.   Let me hear
What you are charged to impart — my father's
  will.

PRIOR.

Heart-cleft by his dear offspring's shame, he
  prays
Your reason be restored, your wayward sense
Renew its due allegiance. For his son
He, the good parent, weeps — hot drops of
  gall,
Wrung from a spirit seldom eased by tears.
But for his honor pricked, the Landgrave
  takes
More just and general vengeance.

PRINCE WILLIAM.

        In the name of God,
What has he done to *her ?*

PRIOR.

Naught, naught, — as yet.

Sweet Prince, be calm ; you leap like flax to
    flame.

You nest within your heart a cockatrice,

Pluck it from out your bosom and breathe pure

Of the filthy egg.   The Landgrave brooks no
    more

The abomination that infects his town.

The Jews of Nordhausen are doomed.

PRINCE WILLIAM.

                          Alack !

Who and how many of that harmless tribe,

Those meek and pious men, have been elected

To glut with innocent blood the oppressor's
    wrath ?

PRIOR.

Who should go free where equal guilt is shared ?

Frederick is just — they perish all at once,

Generous moreover — for in their mode of death

He grants them choice.

PRINCE WILLIAM.

                My father had not lost

The human semblance when I saw him last.

Nor can he be divorced in this short space

From his shrewd wit.   How shall he make pro-
    vision

For the vast widowed, orphaned host this deed
Burdens the state withal?

PRIOR.

                                Oh excellent!
This is the crown of folly, topping all!
Forgive me, Prince, when I gain breath to
        point
Your comic blunder, you will laugh with me.
Patience — I 'll draw my chin as long as yours.
Well, 't was my fault — one should be ac-
        curate —
Jews, said I? when I meant Jews, Jewesses,
And Jewlings! all betwixt the age
Of twenty-four hours, and of five score years.
Of either sex, of every known degree,
All the contaminating vermin purged
With one clean, searching blast of wholesome
        fire.

PRINCE WILLIAM.

O Christ, disgraced, insulted!   Horrible man,
Remembered be your laugh in lowest hell,
Dragging you to the nether pit!   Forgive me;
You are my friend — take me from here — un-
        bolt
Those iron doors — I 'll crawl upon my knees
Unto my father — I have much to tell him.
For but the freedom of one hour, sweet Prior,
I 'll brim the vessels of the Church with gold.

PRIOR.

Boy! your bribes touch not, nor your curses
    shake
The minister of Christ. Yet I will bear
Your message to the Landgrave.

PRINCE WILLIAM.

                Whet your tongue
Keen as the archangel's blade of truth — your
    voice
Be as God's thunder, and your heart one blaze —
Then can you speak my cause. With me, it
    needs
No plausive gift; the smitten head, stopped
    throat,
Blind eyes and silent suppliance of sorrow
Persuade beyond all eloquence. Great God!
Here while I rage and beat against my bars,
The infernal fagots may be stacked for her,
The hell-spark kindled. Go to him, dear Prior,
Speak to him gently, be not too much moved,
'Neath its rude case you had ever a soft heart,
And he is stirred by mildness more than passion.
Recall to him her round, clear, ardent eyes,
The shower of sunshine that's her hair, the sheen
Of the cream-white flesh — shall these things
    serve as fuel?
Tell him that when she heard once he was
    wounded,

And how he bled and anguished ; at the tale
She wept for pity.

PRIOR.

                    If her love be true
She will adore her lover's God, embrace
The faith that marries you in life and death.
This promise with the Landgrave would prevail
More than all sobs and pleadings.

PRINCE WILLIAM.

                              Save her, save her !
If any promise, vow, or oath can serve.
Oh trusting, tranquil Süsskind, who estopped
Your ears forewarned, bandaged your visioned
        eyes,
To woo destruction !   Stay ! did he not speak
Of amulet or talisman ?   These horrors
Have crowded out my wits.   Yea, the gold
        casket !
What fixed serenity beamed from his brow,
Laying the precious box within my hands !

> [*He brings from the shelf the casket, and hands it to
> the Prior.*

Deliver this unto the Prince my father,
Nor lose one vital moment.   What it holds,
I guess not — but my light heart whispers me
The jewel safety's locked beneath its lid.

PRIOR.

First I must foil such devil's tricks as lurk
In its gem-crusted cabinet.

PRINCE WILLIAM.

                    Away!
Deliverance posts on your return.   I feel it.
For your much comfort thanks.   Good-night.

PRIOR.

                              Good-night.
                              [*Exit.*

ACT III.

SCENE I.

A cell in the Wartburg Monastery.   Enter PRIOR PEPPER-
CORN *with the casket.*

PRIOR.

So!   Glittering shell where doubtless shines con-
        cealed
An orient treasure fit to bribe a king,
Ransom a prince and buy him for a son.
I have baptized thee now before the altar,
Effaced the Jew's contaminating touch,
And I am free to claim the Church's tithe
From thy receptacle.
        [*He is about to unlock the casket, when enters Lay-
        Brother, and he hastily conceals it.*

LAY-BROTHER.

                    Peace be thine, father!

PRIOR.

Amen! and thine.   What's new?

LAY BROTHER.

> A strange Flagellant
Fresh come to Wartburg craves a word with
thee.

PRIOR.

Bid him within.
> [*Exit Lay-Brother.* PRIOR *places the casket in a
> Cabinet.*

> Patience!   No hour of the day
Brings freedom to the priest.

Reënter Lay-Brother ushering in NORDMANN, *and exit.*

> Brother, all hail!
Blessed be thou who comest in God's name!

NORDMANN.

May the Lord grant thee thine own prayer four-
fold!

PRIOR.

What is thine errand?

NORDMANN.

> Look at me, my father.
Long since you called me friend.
> [*The* PRIOR *looks at him attentively, while an ex-
> pression of wonder and terror gradually over-
> spreads his face.*

PRIOR.

Almighty God!
The grave gives up her dead. Thou canst not
be —

NORDMANN.

Nordmann of Nordmannstein, the Knight of
Treffurt.

PRIOR.

He was beheaded years agone.

NORDMANN.

His death
Had been decreed, but in his stead a squire
Clad in his garb and masked, paid bloody forfeit.
A loyal wretch on whom the Prince wreaked ven-
geance,
Rather than publish the true bird had flown.

PRIOR.

Does Frederick know thou art in Eisenach?

NORDMANN.

Who would divine the Knight of Nordmannstein
In the Flagellants' weeds? From land to land,
From town to town, we cry, "Death to the
Jews!
Hep! hep! *Hierosolyma est perdita!*"

They die like rats ; in Gotha they are burned ;
Two of the devil brutes in Chatelard,
Child-murderers, wizards, breeders of the Plague,
Had the truth squeezed from them with screws
       and racks,
All with explicit date, place, circumstance,
And written as it fell from dying lips
By scriveners of the law.   On their confession
The Jews of Savoy were destroyed.   To-morrow
       noon
The holy flames shall dance in Nordhausen.

PRIOR.

Your zeal bespeaks you fair. In your deep eyes
A mystic fervor shines ; yet your scarred flesh
And shrunken limbs denote exhausted nature,
Collapsing under discipline.

NORDMANN.
              Speak not
Of the degrading body and its pangs.
I am all zeal, all energy, all spirit.
Jesus was wroth at me, at all the world,
For our indulgence of the flesh, our base
Compounding with his enemies the Jews.
But at Madonna Mary's intercession,
He charged an angel with this gracious word,
" Whoso will scourge himself for forty days,
And labor towards the clean extermination
Of earth's corrupting vermin, shall be saved."

Oh, what vast peace this message brought my
        soul!
I have learned to love the ecstasy of pain.
When the sweat stands upon my flesh, the blood
Throbs in my bursting veins, my twisted muscles
Are cramped with agony, I seem to crawl
Anigh his feet who suffered on the Cross.

PRIOR.

O all transforming Time! Can this be he,
The iron warrior of a decade since,
The gallant youth of earlier years, whose pranks
And reckless buoyancy of temper flashed
Clear sunshine through my gloom?

NORDMANN.

                  I am unchanged
(Save that the spirit of grace has fallen on me).
Urged by one motive through these banished
        years,
Fed by one hope, awake to realize
One living dream — my long delayed revenge.
You saw the day when Henry Schnetzen's castle
Was razed with fire?

PRIOR.

        I saw it.

NORDMANN.

                Schnetzen's wife,
Three days a mother, perished.

PRIOR.

And his child?

NORDMANN.

His child was saved.

PRIOR.

By whom?

NORDMANN.

By the same Jew
Who had betrayed the Castle.

PRIOR.

Süsskind von Orb?

NORDMANN.

Süsskind von Orb! and Schnetzen's daughter
        lives
As the Jew's child within the Judengasse.

PRIOR (*eagerly*).

What proof hast thou of this?

NORDMANN.

Proof of these eyes!
I visited von Orb to ask a loan.
There saw I such a maiden as no Jew
Was ever blessed withal since Jesus died.

White as a dove, with hair like golden floss,
Eyes like an Alpine lake.   The haughty line
Of brow imperial, high bridged nose, fine chin,
Seemed like the shadow cast upon the wall,
Where Lady Schnetzen stood.

PRIOR.

                              Why hast thou ne'er
Discovered her to Schnetzen?

NORDMANN.

                              He was my friend.
I shared with him thirst, hunger, sword, and fire.
But he became a courtier.   When the Margrave
Sent me his second challenge to the field,
His messenger was Schnetzen! 'Mongst his
          knights,
The apple of his eye was Henry Schnetzen.
He was the hound that hunted me to death.
He stood by Frederick's side when I was led,
Bound, to the presence.   I denounced him
          coward,
He smote me on the cheek.   Christ! it stings
          yet.
He hissed — "My liege, let Henry Nordmann
          hang!
He is no knight, for he receives a blow,
Nor dare avenge it!"   My gyved wrists moved
          not,
No nerve twitched in my face, although I felt

Flame leap there from my heart, then flying
    back,
Leave it cold-bathed with deathly ooze — my
    soul
In silence took her supreme vow of hate.

PRIOR.

Praise be to God that thou hast come to-day.
To-morrow were too late.   Hast thou not heard
Frederick sends Schnetzen unto Nordhausen,
With fire and torture for the Jews ?

NORDMANN.

                So ! Henry Schnetzen
Shall be the Jews' destroyer ?   Ah !

PRIOR.

                    One moment.
Mayhap this box which Süsskind sends the
    Prince
Reveals more wonders.

> [*He brings forth the Casket from the Cabinet, opens
> it, and discovers a golden cross and a parchment
> which he hastily overlooks.*

              Hark ! your word 's confirmed
Blessed be Christ, our Lord ! (*reads*).
" I Süsskind von Orb of Nordhausen, swear
by the unutterable Name, that on the day when
the Castle of Salza was burned, I rescued the
infant daughter of Henry Schnetzen from the

flames. I purposed restoring her to her father,
but when I returned to Nordhausen, I found my
own child lying on her bier, and my wife in
fevered frenzy calling for her babe. I sought
the leech, who counselled me to show the Chris-
tian child to the bereaved mother as her own.
The pious trick prevailed; the fever broke, the
mother was restored. But never would she part
with the child, even when she had learned to
whom it belonged, and until she was gathered
with the dead — may peace be with her soul! —
she fostered in our Jewish home the offspring of
the Gentile knight. Then again would I have
yielded the girl to her parent, but Schnetzen was
my foe, and I feared the haughty baron would
disown the daughter who came from the hands
of the Jew. Now however the maiden's tempo-
ral happiness demands that she be acknowledged
by her rightful father. Let him see what I have
written. As a token, behold this golden cross,
bound by the Lady Schnetzen round the infant's
neck. May the God of Abraham, Isaac, and
Jacob redeem and bless me as I have writ the
truth."

PRIOR.

I thank the Saints that this has come betimes.
Thou shalt renounce thy hate. Vengeance is
     mine,
The Lord hath said.

NORDMANN.

O all-transforming Time !
Is this meek, saintly-hypocrite, the firm,
Ambitious, resolute Reinhard Peppercorn,
Terror of Jews and beacon of the Church?
Look, you, I have won the special grace of
    Christ,
He knows through what fierce anguish ! Now he
    leans
Out of his heaven to whisper in mine ear,
And reach me my revenge. He makes my
    cause
His own — and I shall fail upon these heights,
Sink from the level of a hate sublime,
To puerile pity !

PRIOR.

Be advised. You hold
Your enemy's living heart within your hands.
This secret is far costlier than you dreamed,
For Frederick's son wooes Schnetzen's daughter.
    See,
A hundred delicate springs your wit may move,
Your puppets are the Landgrave and the Prince,
The Governor of Salza and the Jews.
You may recover station, wealth, and honor,
Selling your secret shrewdly ; while rash greed
Of clumsy vengeance may but drag you down
In the wild whirl of universal ruin.

NORDMANN.

Christ teach me whom to trust! I would not
    spill
One drop from out this brimming glorious cup
For which my parched heart pants. I will con-
    sider.

PRIOR.

Pardon me now, if I break off our talk.
Let all rest as it stands until the dawn.
I have many orisons before the light.

NORDMANN.

Good-night, true friend. Devote a prayer to me.
(*Aside.*) I will outwit you, serpent, though you
    glide
Athwart the dark, noiseless and swift as fate.

[*Exit.*

SCENE II.

*On the road to Nordhausen. Moonlit, rocky landscape.
On the right between high, white cliffs a narrow stream
spanned by a wooden bridge. Thick bushes and trees.*

Enter PRINCE WILLIAM *and* PAGE.

PRINCE WILLIAM.

Is this the place where we shall find fresh
    steeds?
Would I had not dismounted!

PAGE.

Nay, sir ; beyond
The Werra bridge the horses wait for us.
These rotten planks would never bear their
     weight.

PRINCE WILLIAM.

When I am Landgrave these things shall be
     cared for.
This is an ugly spot for travellers
To loiter in. How swift the water runs,
Brawling above our voices.   Human cries
Would never reach Liborius' convent yonder,
Perched on the sheer, chalk cliff. I think of
     peril,
From my excess of joy.   My spirit chafes,
She that would breast broad-winged the air,
     must halt
On stumbling mortal limbs. Look, thither, boy,
How the black shadows of the tree-boles stripe
The moon-blanched bridge and meadow.

PAGE.

Sir, what 's that ?
Yon stir and glitter in the bush ?

PRINCE WILLIAM.

The moon,
Pricking the dewdrops, plays fantastic tricks

With objects most familiar.   Look again,
And where thou sawst the steel-blue flicker glint,
Thou findst a black, wet leaf.

PAGE.

No, no ! O God !
Your sword, sir !   Treason !

> [*Four armed masked men leap from out the bush, seize,
> bind, and overmaster, after a brief but violent re-
> sistance, the Prince and his servant.*

PRINCE WILLIAM.

Who are ye, villains ? lying
In murderous ambush for the Prince of Meissen ?
If you be knights, speak honorably your names,
And I will combat you in knightly wise.
If ye be robbers, name forthwith your ransom.
Let me but speed upon my journey now.
By Christ's blood !   I beseech you, let me go !
Ho ! treason ! murder ! help !

> [*He is dragged off struggling.   Exeunt omnes.*

SCENE III.

Nordhausen.   A room in SÜSSKIND'S *house.* LIEBHAID
and CLAIRE.

LIEBHAID.

Say on, poor girl, if but to speak these hor-
rors
Revive not too intense a pang.

CLAIRE.

Not so.

For all my woes seem here to merge their flood
Into a sea of infinite repose.
Through France our journey led, as I have told,
From desolation unto desolation.
Naught   stayed   my   father's   course — sword,
          storm, flame, plague,
Exhaustion of the eighty year old frame,
O'ertaxed beyond endurance.   Once, once only,
His   divine   force   succumbed.   'T was   at   day's
          close,
And all the air was one discouragement
Of April snow-flakes.   I was drenched, cold, sick,
With weariness and hunger light of head,
And on the open road, suddenly turned
The whole world like the spinning flakes of snow.
My   numb   hand   slipped   from   his,   and   all   was
          blank.
His beard, his breath upon my brow, his tears
Scalding   my   cheek   hugged   close   against   his
          breast,
And in my ear deep groans awoke me.   "God!"
I heard him cry,   "try me not past my strength.
No prophet I, a blind, old dying man!"
Gently I drew his face to mine, and kissed,
Whispering courage — then his spirit broke
Utterly; shattered were his wits, I feared.
But past is past; he is at peace, and I

Find shelter from the tempest.   Tell me rather
Of your serene life.

LIEBHAID.

                    Happiness is mute.
What record speaks of placid, golden days,
Matched each with each as twins? Till yester
          eve
My life was simple as a song.   At whiles
Dark tales have reached us of our people's
          wrongs,
Strange, far-off anguish, furrowing with fresh
          care
My father's brow, draping our home with gloom.
We were still blessed; the Landgrave is his
          friend —
The Prince — my Prince — dear Claire, ask me
          no more!
My adored enemy, my angel-fiend,
Splitting my heart against my heart!   O God,
How shall I pray for strength to love him less
Than mine own soul?

CLAIRE.

                    What mean these contrary words?
These passionate tears?

LIEBHAID.

                    Brave girl, who art inured
To difficult privation and rude pain,

What good shall come forswearing kith and God,
To follow the allurements of the heart?

CLAIRE.

Duty wears one face, but a thousand masks.
Thy feet she leads to glittering peaks, while mine
She guides midst brambled roadways.   Not the
        first
Art thou of Israel's women, chosen of God,
To rule o'er rulers.   I remember me
A verse my father often would repeat
Out of our sacred Talmud : " Every time
The sun, moon, stars begin again their course,
They hesitate, trembling and filled with shame,
Blush at the blasphemous worship offered them,
And each time God's voice thunders, crying out,
On with your duty ! "

Enter REUBEN.

REUBEN.

                    Sister, we are lost !
The streets are thronged with panic-stricken folk.
Wild rumors fill the air.   Two of our tribe,
Young Mordecai, as I hear, and old Baruch,
Seized by the mob, were dragged towards Eise-
        nach,
Cruelly used, left to bleed out their lives,
In the wayside ditch at night.   This morn, be-
        times,

The iron-hearted Governor of Salza
Rides furious into Nordhausen; his horse,
Spurred past endurance, drops before the gate.
The Council has been called to hear him read
The Landgrave's message, — all men say, 't is death
    Unto our race.

LIEBHAID.

    Where is our father, Reuben?

REUBEN.

With Rabbi Jacob. Through the streets they walk,
Striving to quell the terror. Ah, too late!
Had he but heeded the prophetic voice,
This warning angel led to us in vain!

LIEBHAID.

Brother, be calm. Man your young heart to front
Whatever ills the Lord afflicts us with.
What does Prince William? Hastes he not to aid?

REUBEN.

None know his whereabouts. Some say he 's held
Imprisoned by the Landgrave. Others tell
While he was posting with deliverance
To Nordhausen, in bloody Schnetzen's wake,

He was set upon by ruffians — kidnapped —
    killed.
What do I know — hid till our ruin 's wrought.
              [LIEBHAID *swoons.*

CLAIRE.

Hush, foolish boy. See how your rude words
    hurt.
Look up, sweet girl ; take comfort.

REUBEN.

              Pluck up heart :
Dear sister, pardon me ; he lives, he lives !

LIEBHAID.

God help me ! Shall my heart crack for love's
    loss
That meekly bears my people's martyrdom ?
He lives — I feel it — to live or die with me.
I love him as my soul — no more of that.
I am all Israel's now — till this cloud pass,
I have no thought, no passion, no desire,
Save for my people.

Enter SÜSSKIND.

SÜSSKIND.

            Blessed art thou, my child !
This is the darkest hour before the dawn.
Thou art the morning-star of Israel.

How dear thou art to me — heart of my heart,
Mine, mine, all mine to-day! the pious thought,
The orient spirit mine, the Jewish soul.
The glowing veins that sucked life-nourishment
From Hebrew mother's milk.   Look at me, Lieb-
     haid,
Tell me you love me.   Pity me, my God!
No fiercer pang than this did Jephthah know.

LIEBHAID.

Father, what wild and wandering words are
    these?
Is all hope lost?

SÜSSKIND.

           Nay, God is good to us.
I am so well assured the town is safe,
That I can weep my private loss — of thee.
An ugly dream I had, quits not my sense,
That you, made Princess of Thuringia,
Forsook your father, and forswore your race.
Forgive me, Liebhaid, I am calm again,
We must be brave — I who besought my tribe
To bide their fate in Nordhausen, and you
Whom God elects for a peculiar lot.
With many have I talked; some crouched at
    home,
Some wringing hands about the public ways.
I gave all comfort.   I am very weary.
My children, we had best go in and pray,
Solace and safety dwell but in the Lord.

                         [*Exeunt.*

ACT IV.

SCENE I.

The City Hall at Nordhausen. Deputies and Burghers assembling. To the right, at a table near the President's chair, is seated the Public Scrivener. Enter DIETRICH VON TETTENBORN, *and* HENRY SCHNETZEN *with an open letter in his hand.*

SCHNETZEN.

Didst hear the fellow's words who handed it?
I asked from whom it came, he spoke by rote,
" The pepper bites, the corn is ripe for harvest,
I come from Eisenach."   'T is some tedious jest.

TETTENBORN.

Doubtless your shrewd friend Prior Peppercorn
Masks here some warning.   Ask the scrivener
To help us to its contents.

SCHNETZEN (*to the clerk*).

Read me these.

SCRIVENER (*reads*).

" Beware, Lord Henry Schnetzen, of Süsskind's lying tongue !   He will thrust a cuckoo's egg into your nest.

[Signed]   ONE WHO KNOWS."

SCHNETZEN.

A cuckoo's egg! that riddle puzzles me ;
But this I know.   Schnetzen is no man's dupe,
Much less a Jew's.

[SCHNETZEN *and* VON TETTENBORN *take their seats
side by side.*

TETTENBORN.

Knights, counsellors and burghers !
Sir Henry Schnetzen, Governor of Salza,
Comes on grave mission from His Highness
      Frederick,
Margrave of Meissen, Landgrave of Thuringia,
Our town's imperial Patron and Protector.

SCHNETZEN.

Gentles, I greet you in the Landgrave's name,
The honored bearer of his princely script,
Sealed with his signet. Read, good Master
      Clerk.

[*He hands a parchment to the Scrivener, who reads
aloud :*

Lord President and Deputies of the town of
Nordhausen!   Know that we, Frederick, Mar-
grave of Meissen, and Landgrave of Thuringia,
command to be burned all the Jews within our
territories as far as our lands extend, on account
of the great crime they have committed against
Christendom in throwing poison into the wells, of

the truth of which indictment we have absolute
knowledge. Therefore we admonish you to have
the Jews killed in honor of God, so that Chris-
tendom be not. enfeebled by them. Whatever
responsibility you incur, we will assume with our
Lord the Emperor, and with all other lords.
Know also that we send to you Henry Schnetzen,
our Governor of Salza, who shall publicly accuse
your Jews of the above-mentioned crime. There-
fore we beseech you to help him to do justice
upon them, and we will singularly reward your
good will.

Given at Eisenach, the Thursday after St.
Walpurgis, under our secret seal.[1]

A COUNSELLOR (DIETHER VON WERTHER).

Fit silence welcomes this unheard-of wrong !
So ! Ye are men — free, upright, honest men,
Not hired assassins ?   I half doubted it,
Seeing you lend these infamous words your ears.

SCHNETZEN.

Consider, gentlemen of Nordhausen,
Ere ye give heed to the rash partisan.
Ye cross the Landgrave — well ? he crosses you.
It may be I shall ride to Nordhausen,
Not with a harmless script, but with a sword,
And so denounce the town for perjured vow.
What was the Strasburg citizens' reward

---

[1] This is an authentic document.

Who championed these lost wretches, in the face
Of King and Kaiser — three against the world,
Conrad von Winterthur the Burgomaster,
Deputy Gosse Sturm, and Peter Schwarber,
Master Mechanic ?   These leagued fools essayed
To stand between the people's sacred wrath,
And its doomed object.   Well, the Jews, no less,
Were rooted from the city neck and crop,
And their three friends degraded from their
    rank
I' the city council, glad to save their skins.
The Jews are foes to God.   Our Holy Father
Thunders his ban from Rome against all such
As aid the poisoners.   Your oath to God,
And to the Prince enjoins — Death to the Jews.

A BURGHER (REINHARD ROLAPP).

Why all this vain debate ?   The Landgrave's
    brief
Affirms the Jews fling poison in the wells.
Shall we stand by and leave them unmolested,
Till they have made our town a wilderness ?
I say, Death to the Jews !

A BURGHER (HUGO SCHULTZ).

           My lord and brethren,
I have scant gift of speech, ye are all my elders.
Yet hear me for truth's sake, and liberty's.
The Landgrave of Thuringia is our patron,
True — and our town's imperial Governor,

But are we not free burghers? Shall we not
Debate and act in freedom? If Lord Schnetzen
Will force our council with the sword — enough!
We are not frightened schoolboys crouched be-
      neath
The master's rod, but men who bear the sword
As brave as he. By this grim messenger.
Send back this devilish missive. Say to Fred-
      erick
Nordhausen never was enfeoffed to him.
Prithee, Lord President, bid Henry Schnetzen
Withdraw awhile, that we may all take counsel,
According to the hour's necessity,
As free men, whom nor fear nor favor swerves.

TETTENBORN.

Bold youth, you err. True, Nordhausen is free,
And God be witness, we for fear or favor,
Would never shed the blood of innocence.
But here the Prince condemns the Jews to death
For capital crime. Who sees a snake must kill,
Ere it spit fatal venom. I, too, say
Death to the Jews!

ALL.

Death to the Jews! God wills it!

TETTENBORN.

Give me your voices in the urn.
(*The votes are taken.*)   One voice

For mercy, all the rest for death. (*To an Usher.*)
  Go thou
To the Jews' quarter; bid Süsskind von Orb,
And Rabbi Jacob hither to the Senate,
To hear the Landgrave's and the town's decree.
        [*Exit Usher.*
(*To Schnetzen.*) What learn you of this evil
  through the State?

SCHNETZEN.

It swells to monstrous bulk. In many towns,
Folk build high ramparts round the wells and
  springs.
In some they shun the treacherous sparkling
  brooks,
To drink dull rain-water, or melted snow,
In mountain districts. Frederick has been pa-
  tient,
And too long clement, duped by fleece-cloaked
  wolves.
But now his subjects' clamor rouses him
To front the general peril. As I hear,
A fiendish and far-reaching plot involves
All Christian thrones and peoples. These vile
  vermin,
Burrowing underneath society,
Have leagued with Moors in Spain, with heretics
Too plentiful — Christ knows! in every land,
And planned a subterraneous, sinuous scheme,
To overthrow all Christendom. But see,

Where with audacious brows, and steadfast mien,
They enter, bold as innocence.   Now listen,
For we shall hear brave falsehoods.

Enter Süsskind von Orb *and* Rabbi Jacob.

TETTENBORN.

Rabbi Jacob,
And thou, Süsskind von Orb, bow down, and
     learn
The Council's pleasure.   You the least despised
By true believers, and most reverenced
By your own tribe, we grace with our free leave
To enter, yea, to lift your voices here,
Amid these wise and honorable men,
If ye find aught to plead, that mitigates
The just severity of your doom.   Our prince,
Frederick the Grave, Patron of Nordhausen,
Ordains that all the Jews within his lands,
For the foul crime of poisoning the wells,
Bringing the Black Death upon Christendom,
Shall be consumed with flame.

RABBI JACOB (*springing forward and clasping his
          hands*).

I' the name of God,
Your God and ours, have mercy !

SÜSSKIND.

Noble lords,
Burghers, and artisans of Nordhausen,

Wise, honorable, just, God-fearing men,
Shall ye condemn or ever ye have heard?
Sure, one at least owns here the close, kind
      name
Of Brother — unto him I turn.   At least
Some sit among you who have wedded wives,
Bear the dear title and the precious charge
Of Husband — unto these I speak.   Some here,
Are crowned, it may be, with the sacred name
Of Father — unto these I pray.   All, all
Are sons — all have been children, all have
      known
The love of parents — unto these I cry:
Have mercy on us, we are innocent,
Who are brothers, husbands, fathers, sons as ye!
Look you, we have dwelt among you many years,
Led thrifty, peaceable, well-ordered lives.
Who can attest, who prove we ever wrought
Or ever did devise the smallest harm,
Far less this fiendish crime against the State?
Rather let those arise who owe the Jews
Some debt of unpaid kindness, profuse alms,
The Hebrew leech's serviceable skill,
Who know our patience under injury,
And ye would see, if all stood bravely forth,
A motley host, led by the Landgrave's self,
Recruited from all ranks, and in the rear,
The humblest, veriest wretch in Nordhausen.
We know the Black Death is a scourge of God.
Is not our flesh as capable of pain,

Our blood as quick envenomed as your own?
Has the Destroying Angel passed the posts
Of Jewish doors — to visit Christian homes?
We all are slaves of one tremendous Hour.
We drink the waters which our enemies say
We spoil with poison, — we must breathe, as ye,
The universal air, — we droop, faint, sicken,
From the same causes to the selfsame end.
Ye are not strangers to me, though ye wear
Grim masks to-day — lords, knights and citi-
     zens,
Few do I see whose hand has pressed not mine,
In cordial greeting.   Dietrich von Tettenborn,
If at my death my wealth be confiscate
Unto the State, bethink you, lest she prove
A harsher creditor than I have been.
Stout Meister Rolapp, may you never again
Languish so nigh to death that Simon's art
Be needed to restore your lusty limbs.
Good Hugo Schultz — ah! be those blessed tears
Remembered unto you in Paradise!
Look there, my lords, one of your council weeps,
If you be men, why, then an angel sits
On yonder bench. You have good cause to weep,
You who are Christian, and disgraced in that
Whereof you made your boast. I have no tears.
A fiery wrath has scorched their source, a voice
Shrills through my brain — "Not upon us, on
     them
Fall everlasting woe, if this thing be!"

SCHNETZEN.

My lords of Nordhausen, shall ye be stunned
With sounding words? Behold the serpent's
    skin,
Sleek-shining, clear as sunlight; yet his tooth
Holds deadly poison. Even as the Jews
Did nail the Lord of heaven on the Cross,
So will they murder all his followers,
When once they have the might. Beware, be-
    ware!

SÜSSKIND.

So *you* are the accuser, my lord Schnetzen?
Now I confess, before you I am guilty.
You are in all this presence, the one man
Whom any Jew hath wronged — and I that Jew.
Oh, my offence is grievous; punish me
With the utmost rigor of the law, for theft
And violence, whom ye deemed an honest man,
But leave my tribe unharmed! I yield my
    hands
Unto your chains, my body to your fires;
Let one life serve for all.

SCHNETZEN.

                You hear, my lords,
How the prevaricating villain shrinks
From the absolute truth, yet dares not front his
    Maker
With the full damnable lie hot on his lips.

Not thou alone, my private foe, shalt die,
But all thy race.   Thee had my vengeance
    reached,
Without appeal to Prince or citizen.
Silence ! my heart is cuirassed as my breast.

RABBI JACOB.

Bear with us, gracious lords ! My friend is
    stunned.
He is an honest man.   Even I, as 't were,
Am stupefied by this surprising news.
Yet, let me think — it seems it is not new,
This is an ancient, well-remembered pain.
What, brother, came not one who prophesied
This should betide exactly as it doth?
That was a shrewd old man ! Your pardon,
    lords,
I think you know not just what you would do.
You say the Jews shall burn — shall burn you
    say ;
Why, good my lords, the Jews are not a flock
Of gallows-birds, they are a colony
Of kindly, virtuous folk.   Come home with me ;
I 'll show you happy hearths, glad roofs, pure
    lives.
Why, some of them are little quick-eyed boys,
Some, pretty, ungrown maidens — children's
    children
Of those who called me to the pastorate.
And some are beautiful tall girls, some, youths

Of marvellous promise, some are old and sick,
Amongst them there be mothers, infants, brides,
Just like your Christian people, for all the world.
Know ye what burning is ?   Hath one of you
Scorched ever his soft flesh, or singed his beard,
His hair, his eyebrows — felt the keen, fierce nip
Of the pungent flame — and raises not his voice
To stop this holocaust?   God! 't is too horrible!
Wake me, my friends, from this terrific dream.

SÜSSKIND.

Courage, my brother.   On our firmness hangs
The dignity of Israel.   Sir Governor,
I have a secret word to speak with you.

SCHNETZEN.

Ye shall enjoy with me the jest.   These knaves
Are apt to quick invention as in crime.
Speak out — I have no secrets from my peers.

SÜSSKIND.

My lord, what answer would you give your
        Christ
If peradventure, in this general doom
You sacrifice a Christian?   Some strayed dove
Lost from your cote, among our vultures caged?
Beware, for midst our virgins there is one
Owes kinship nor allegiance to our tribe.
For her dear sake be pitiful, my lords,
Have mercy on our women !   Spare at least

My daughter Liebhaid, she is none of mine!
She is a Christian!

SCHNETZEN.

Just as I foretold!
The wretches will forswear the sacred'st ties,
Cringing for life.   Serpents, ye all shall die.
So wills the Landgrave; so the court affirms.
Your daughter shall be first, whose wanton arts
Have brought destruction on a princely house.

SÜSSKIND.

My lord, be moved.   You kill your flesh and
        blood.
By *Adonai* I swear, your dying wife
Entrusted to these arms her child.   'T was I
Carried your infant from your burning home.
Lord Schnetzen, will you murder your own
        child?

SCHNETZEN.

Ha, excellent!   I was awaiting this.
Thou wilt inoculate our knightly veins
With thy corrupted Jewish blood.   Thou 'lt foist
This adder on my bosom.   Henry Schnetzen
Is no weak dupe, whom every lie may start.
Make ready, Jew, for death — and warn thy
        tribe.

SÜSSKIND (*kneeling*).

Is there a God in heaven?   I who ne'er knelt

Until this hour to any man on earth,
Tyrant, before thee I abase myself.
If one red drop of human blood still flow
In thy congealed veins, if thou e'er have known
Touch of affection, the blind natural instinct
Of common kindred, even beasts partake,
Thou man of frozen stone, thou hollow statue,
Grant me one prayer, that thou wilt look on
    her.
Then shall the eyes of thy dead wife gaze back
From out the maiden's orbs, then shall a voice
Within thine entrails, cry — This is my child.

SCHNETZEN.

Enough! I pray you, my lord President,
End this unseemly scene. This wretched Jew
Would thrust a cuckoo's egg within my nest.
I have had timely warning. Send the twain
Back to their people, that the court's decree
Be published unto all.

SÜSSKIND.

          Lord Tettenborn!
Citizens! will you see this nameless crime
Brand the clean earth, blacken the crystal
    heaven?
Why, no man stirs! God! with what thick
    strange fumes
Hast thou, o' the sudden, brutalized their sense?
Or am I mad? Is this already hell?

Worshipful fiends, I have good store of gold,
Packed in my coffers, or loaned out to — Chris-
      tians;
I give it you as free as night bestows
Her copious dews — my life shall seal the bond,
Have mercy on my race!

TETTENBORN.

                 No more, no more!
Go, bid your tribe make ready for their death
At sunset.

RABBI JACOB.

      Oh!

SÜSSKIND.

           At set of sun to-day?
Why, if you travelled to the nighest town,
Summoned to stand before a mortal Prince,
You would need longer grace to put in order
Household effects, to bid farewell to friends,
And make yourself right worthy.   But our way
Is long, our journey difficult, our judge
Of awful majesty.   Must we set forth,
Haste-flushed and unprepared?   One brief day
      more,
And all my wealth is yours!

TETTENBORN.

            We have heard enough.
Begone, and bear our message.

SÜSSKIND.

       Courage, brother,
Our fate is sealed. These tigers are athirst.
Return we to our people to proclaim
The gracious sentence of the noble court.
Let us go thank the Lord who made us those
To suffer, not to do, this deed. Be strong.
So ! lean on me — we have little time to lose.
           [*Exeunt.*

ACT. V.

SCENE I.

A Room in Süsskind's House. LIEBHAID, CLAIRE,
    REUBEN.

LIEBHAID.

The air hangs sultry as in mid-July.
Look forth, Claire ; moves not some big thunder-
  cloud
Athwart the sky ? My heart is sick.

CLAIRE.

        Nay, Liebhaid.
The clear May sun is shining, and the air
Blows fresh and cordial from the budding hills.

LIEBHAID.

Reuben, what is 't o'clock. Our father stays.
The midday meal was cold an hour agone.

REUBEN.

'T is two full hours past noon; he should be
    here.
Ah see, he comes.   Great God! what woe has
    chanced?
He totters on his staff; he has grown old
Since he went forth this morn.

(*Enter* SÜSSKIND.)

LIEBHAID.

Father, what news?

SÜSSKIND.

The Lord have mercy!   Vain is the help of
    man.
Children, is all in order?   We must start
At set of sun on a long pilgrimage.
So wills the Landgrave, so the court decrees.

LIEBHAID.

What is it, father?   Exile?

SÜSSKIND.

Yea, just that.
We are banished from our vexed, uncertain
    homes,
'Midst foes and strangers, to a land of peace,
Where joy abides, where only comfort is.
Banished from care, fear, trouble, life — to
    death.

REUBEN.

Oh horror! horror!   Father, I will not die.
Come, let us flee — we yet have time for
        flight.
I 'll bribe the sentinel — he will ope the gates.
Liebhaid, Claire, Father! let us flee!   Away
To some safe land where we may nurse revenge.

SÜSSKIND.

Courage, my son, and peace.   We may not
        flee.
Didst thou not see the spies who dogged my
        steps?
The gates are thronged with citizens and guards.
We must not flee — God wills that we should die.

LIEBHAID.

Said you at sunset?

SÜSSKIND.

                So they have decreed.

CLAIRE.

Oh why not now?   Why spare the time to
        warn?
Why came they not with thee to massacre,
Leaving no agony betwixt the sentence
And instant execution?   That were mercy!
Oh, my prophetic father!

SÜSSKIND.

They allow
Full five hours' grace to shrive our souls with
    prayer.
We shall assemble in the Synagogue,
As on Atonement Day, confess our sins,
Recite the Kaddish for the Dead, and chant
Our Shibboleth, the Unity of God,
Until the supreme hour when we shall stand
Before the mercy-seat.

LIEBHAID.

In what dread shape
Approaches death?

SÜSSKIND.

Nerve your young hearts, my children.
We shall go down as God's three servants went
Into the fiery furnace.   Not again
Shall the flames spare the true-believers' flesh.
The anguish shall be fierce and strong, yet brief.
Our spirits shall not know the touch of pain,
Pure as refined gold they shall issue safe
From the hot crucible; a pleasing sight
Unto the Lord.   Oh, 't is a rosy bed
Where we shall couch, compared with that
    whereon
They lie who kindle this accursed blaze.
Ye shrink? ye would avert your martyred brows

From the immortal crowns the angels offer?
What! are we Jews and are afraid of death?
God's chosen people, shall we stand a-tremble
Before our Father, as the Gentiles use?

REUBEN.

Shall the smoke choke us, father? or the flame
Consume our flesh?

SÜSSKIND.

       I know not, boy.   Be sure
The Lord will temper the shrewd pain for those
Who trust in Him.

REUBEN.

       May I stand by thy side,
And hold my hand in thine until the end?

SÜSSKIND.

(*Aside.*) What solace hast thou, God, in all thy
       heavens
For such an hour as this?   Yea, hand in hand
We walk, my son, through fire, to meet the
       Lord.
Yet there is one among us shall not burn.
A secret shaft long rankling in my heart,
Now I withdraw, and die.   Our general doom,
Liebhaid, is not for thee.   Thou art no Jewess.
Thy father is the man who wills our death;
Lord Henry Schnetzen.

LIEBHAID.

Look at me! your eyes
Are sane, correcting your distracted words.
This is Love's trick, to rescue me from death.
My love is firm as thine, and dies with thee.

CLAIRE.

Oh, Liebhaid, live. Hast thou forgot the
      Prince?
Think of the happy summer blooms for thee
When we are in our graves.

LIEBHAID.

And I shall smile,
Live and rejoice in love, when ye are dead?

SÜSSKIND.

My child, my child! By the Ineffable Name,
The Adonai, I swear, thou must believe,
Albeit thy father scoffed, gave me the lie.
Go kneel to him — for if he see thy face,
Or hear thy voice, he shall not doubt, but save.

LIEBHAID.

Never! If I be offspring to that kite,
I here deny my race, forsake my father, —
So does thy dream fall true. Let him save thee,
Whose hand has guided mine, whose lips have
      blessed,

Whose bread has nourished me. Thy God is
      mine,
Thy people are my people.

VOICES (*without*).

Süsskind von Orb!

SÜSSKIND.

I come, my friends.

Enter boisterously certain Jews.

1ST JEW.

Come to the house of God!

2D JEW.

Wilt thou desert us for whose sake we perish?

3D JEW.

The awful hour draws nigh. Come forth with us
Unto the Synagogue.

SÜSSKIND.

Bear with me, neighbors.
Here we may weep, here for the last time know
The luxury of sorrow, the soft touch
Of natural tenderness ; here our hearts may
      break ;
Yonder no tears, no faltering !   Eyes serene
Lifted to heaven, and defiant brows
To those who have usurped the name of men,

Must prove our faith and valor limitless
As is their cruelty.   One more embrace,
My daughter, thrice my daughter!   Thine affec-
      tion
Outshines the hellish flames of hate ; farewell,
But for a while ; beyond the river of fire
I 'll fold thee in mine arms, immortal angel!
For thee, poor orphan, soon to greet again
The blessed brows of parents, I dreamed not
The grave was all the home I had to give.
Go thou with Liebhaid, and array yourselves
As for a bridal.   Come, little son, with me.
Friends, I am ready.   O my God, my God,
Forsake us not in our extremity !

                    [*Exeunt* Süsskind *and* Jews.

SCENE II.

*A Street in the Judengasse.   Several Jews pass across the
      stage, running and with gestures of distress.*

JEWS.

Woe, woe! the curse has fallen !   [*Exeunt.*

Enter other Jews.

1ST JEW.

                    We are doomed.
The fury of the Lord has smitten us.
Oh that mine head were waters and mine eyes
Fountains of tears ![1]   God has forsaken us.

                  [*They knock at the doors of the houses.*

[1] Jeremiah ix. 1.

2D JEW.

What, Benjamin! Open the door to death!
We all shall die at sunset!   Menachem!
Come forth! Come forth! Manasseh! Daniel!
   Ezra!

> [*Jews appear at the windows.*

ONE CALLING FROM ABOVE.

Neighbors, what wild alarm is this?

1ST JEW.

                              Descend!
Descend!   Come with us to the house of prayer.
Save himself whoso can! we all shall burn.

> [*Men and women appear at the doors of the houses.*

ONE OF THE MEN AT THE DOOR.

Beseech you brethren, calmly.   Tell us all!
Mine aged father lies at point of death
Gasping within.   Ye'll thrust him in his grave
With boisterous clamor.

1ST JEW.

                         Blessed is the man
Whom the Lord calls unto Himself in peace!
Süsskind von Orb and Rabbi Jacob come
From the tribunal where the vote is — Death
To all our race.

SEVERAL VOICES.

Woe! woe!   God pity us!

1ST JEW.

Hie ye within, and take a last farewell
Of home, love, life — put on your festal robes.
So wills the Rabbi, and come forth at once
To pray till sunset in the Synagogue.

AN OLD MAN.

O God!   Is this the portion of mine age?
Were my white hairs, my old bones spared for
    this?
Oh cruel, cruel!

A YOUNG GIRL.

I am too young to die.
Save me, my father!   To-morrow should have
    been
The feast at Rachel's house.   I longed for that,
Counted the days, dreaded some trivial chance
Might cross my pleasure — Lo, this horror
    comes!

A BRIDE.

Oh love! oh thou just-tasted cup of joy
Snatched from my lips!   Shall we twain lie with
    death,
Dark, silent, cold — whose every sense was
    tuned

To happiness!   Life was too beautiful —
That was the dream — how soon we are awake!
Ah, we have that within our hearts defies
Their fiercest flames.   No end, no end, no end!

JEW.

God with a mighty hand, a stretched-out arm,[1]
And poured-out fury, ruleth over us.
The sword is furbished, sharp i' the slayer's
        hand.
Cry out and howl, thou son of Israel!
Thou shalt be fuel to the fire; thy blood
Shall overflow the land, and thou no more
Shalt be remembered — so the Lord hath spoken.

[Exeunt omnes.

SCENE III.

*Within the Synagogue.   Above in the gallery, women sump-
tuously attired; some with children by the hand or infants
in their arms.   Below the men and boys with silken scarfs
about their shoulders.*

RABBI JACOB.

The Lord is nigh unto the broken heart.[2]
Out of the depths we cry to thee, oh God!
Show us the path of everlasting life;
For in thy presence is the plenitude
Of joy, and in thy right hand endless bliss.

[1] Ezekiel xx. 33; xxi. 11–32.
[2] Service for Day of Atonement.

Enter Süsskind, Reuben, *etc.*

SEVERAL VOICES.

Woe unto us who perish!

A JEW.

     Süsskind von Orb,
Thou hast brought down this doom.   Would we
  had heard
The prophet's voice!

SÜSSKIND.

     Brethren, my cup is full!
Oh let us die as warriors of the Lord.
The Lord is great in Zion.   Let our death
Bring no reproach to Jacob, no rebuke
To Israel.   Hark ye! let us crave one boon
At our assassins' hands; beseech them build
Within God's acre where our fathers sleep,
A dancing-floor to hide the fagots stacked.
Then let the minstrels strike the harp and lute,
And we will dance and sing above the pile,
Fearless of death, until the flames engulf,
Even as David danced before the Lord,
As Miriam danced and sang beside the sea.
Great is our Lord!   His name is glorious
In Judah, and extolled in Israel!
In Salem is his tent, his dwelling place
In Zion; let us chant the praise of God!

A JEW.

Süsskind, thou speakest well! We will meet
death
With dance and song. Embrace him as a bride.
So that the Lord receive us in His tent.

SEVERAL VOICES.

Amen! amen! amen! we dance to death!

RABBI JACOB.

Süsskind, go forth and beg this grace of them.

[*Exit Süsskind.*

Punish us not in wrath, chastise us not
In anger, oh our God! Our sins o'erwhelm
Our smitten heads, they are a grievous load;
We look on our iniquities, we tremble,
Knowing our trespasses. Forsake us not.
Be thou not far from us. Haste to our aid,
Oh God, who art our Saviour and our Rock!

Reënter SÜSSKIND.

SÜSSKIND.

Brethren, our prayer, being the last, is granted.
The hour approaches. Let our thoughts ascend
From mortal anguish to the ecstasy
Of martyrdom, the blessed death of those
Who perish in the Lord. I see, I see
How Israel's ever-crescent glory makes

These flames that would eclipse it, dark as blots
Of candle-light against the blazing sun.
We die a thousand deaths, — drown, bleed, and
        burn ;
Our ashes are dispersed unto the winds.
Yet the wild winds cherish the sacred seed,
The waters guard it in their crystal heart,
The fire refuseth to consume.   It springs,
A tree immortal, shadowing many lands,
Unvisited, unnamed, undreamed as yet.
Rather a vine, full-flowered, golden-branched,
Ambrosial-fruited, creeping on the earth,
Trod by the passer's foot, yet chosen to deck
Tables of princes.   Israel now has fallen
Into the depths, he shall be great in time.[1]
Even as we die in honor, from our death
Shall bloom a myriad heroic lives,
Brave through our bright example, virtuous
Lest our great memory fall in disrepute.
Is one among us brothers, would exchange
His doom against our tyrants, — lot for lot ?
Let him go forth and live — he is no Jew,
Is one who would not die in Israel
Rather than live in Christ, — their Christ who
        smiles
On such a deed as this ?   Let him go forth —

---

[1] The vine creeps on the earth, trodden by the passer's
foot, but its fruit goes upon the table of princes.   Israel
now has fallen in the depths, but he shall be great in the
fullness of time. — TALMUD.

He may die full of years upon his bed.
Ye who nurse rancor haply in your hearts,
Fear ye we perish unavenged?   Not so!
To-day, no! nor to-morrow! but in God's time,
Our witnesses arise.   Ours is the truth,
Ours is the power, the gift of Heaven.   We
      hold
His Law, His lamp, His covenant, His pledge.
Wherever in the ages shall arise
Jew-priest, Jew-poet, Jew-singer, or Jew-saint —
And everywhere I see them star the gloom —
In each of these the martyrs are avenged!

RABBI JACOB.

Bring from the Ark the bell-fringed, silken-
      bound
Scrolls of the Law.   Gather the silver vessels,
Dismantle the rich curtains of the doors,
Bring the Perpetual Lamp; all these shall burn,
For Israel's light is darkened, Israel's Law
Profaned by strangers.   Thus the Lord hath
      said:[1]
"The weapon formed against thee shall not
      prosper,
The tongue that shall contend with thee in judg-
      ment,
Thou shalt condemn.   This is the heritage
Of the Lord's servants and their righteousness.
For thou shalt come to peoples yet unborn,
Declaring that which He hath done.   Amen!"

[1] Conclusion of service for Day of Atonement.

[*The doors of the Synagogue are burst open with
tumultuous noise.   Citizens and officers rush in.*

CITIZENS.

Come forth! the sun sets.   Come, the Council
    waits!
What! will ye teach your betters patience?
    Out!
The Governor is ready.   Forth with you,
Curs! serpents! Judases!   The bonfire burns!
                      [*Exeunt.*

SCENE IV.

*A Public Place.   Crowds of Citizens assembled.   On a
platform are seated* DIETRICH VON TETTENBORN *and*
HENRY SCHNETZEN *with other Members of the Council.*

1ST CITIZEN.

Here's such a throng!   Neighbor, your elbow
    makes
An ill prod for my ribs.

2D CITIZEN.

                I am pushed and squeezed.
My limbs are not mine own.

3D CITIZEN.

                Look this way, wife.
They will come hence, — a pack of just-whipped
    curs.
I warrant you the stiff-necked brutes repent
To-day if ne'er before.

WIFE.

                    I am all a-quiver.
I have seen monstrous sights, — an uncaged
        wolf,
The corpse of one sucked by a vampyre,
The widow Kupfen's malformed child — but
        never
Until this hour, a Jew.

3D CITIZEN.

                    D' ye call me Jew?
Where do you spy one now?

WIFE.

                    You 'll have your jest
Now or anon, what matters it?

4TH CITIZEN.

                    Well, I
Have seen a Jew, and seen one burn at that;
Hard by in Wartburg; he had killed a child.
Zounds! how the serpent wriggled! I smell
        now
The roasting, stinking flesh!

BOY.

                    Father, be these
The folk who murdered Jesus?

4TH CITIZEN.

Ay, my boy.

Remember that, and when you hear them come,
I 'll lift you on my shoulders.   You can fling
Your pebbles with the rest.   [*Trumpets sound.*

CITIZENS.

The Jews! the Jews!

BOY.

Quick, father! lift me!   I see nothing here
But hose and skirts.

[*Music of a march approaching.*

CITIZENS.

What mummery is this?
The sorcerers brew new mischief.

ANOTHER CITIZEN.

Why, they come
Pranked for a holiday; not veiled for death.

ANOTHER CITIZEN.

Insolent braggarts!   They defy the Christ!

Enter, in procession to music, the Jews.   First, RABBI
    JACOB — *after him, sick people, carried on litters* — *then
    old men and women, followed promiscuously by men,
    women, and children of all ages.   Some of the men carry
    gold and silver vessels, some the Rolls of the Law.   One*

bears the Perpetual Lamp, another the Seven-branched silver Candlestick of the Synagogue. The mothers have their children by the hand or in their arms. All richly attired.

CITIZENS.

The misers! they will take their gems and gold
Down to the grave!

CITIZEN'S WIFE.

      So these be Jews!   Christ save us!
To think the devils look like human folk!

CITIZENS.

Cursed be the poison-mixers!   Let them burn!

CITIZENS.

Burn! burn!

Enter SÜSSKIND VON ORB, LIEBHAID, REUBEN, *and*
CLAIRE.

SCHNETZEN.

      Good God! what maid is that?

TETTENBORN.

Liebhaid von Orb.

SCHNETZEN.

      The devil's trick!
He has bewitched mine eyes.

SÜSSKIND (*as he passes the platform*).

Woe to the father
Who murders his own child !

SCHNETZEN.

I am avenged,
Süsskind von Orb !   Blood for blood, fire for fire,
And death for death !
[*Exeunt* SÜSSKIND, LIEBHAID, *etc.*

Enter Jewish youths and maidens.

YOUTHS (*in chorus*).

Let us rejoice, for it is promised us
That we shall enter in God's tabernacle !

MAIDENS.

Our feet shall stand within thy gates, O Zion,
Within thy portals, O Jerusalem !   [*Exeunt.*

CITIZEN'S WIFE.

I can see naught from here.   Let's follow, Hans.

CITIZEN.

Be satisfied.   There is no inch of space
For foot to rest on yonder.   Look ! look there !
How the flames rise !

BOY.

O father, I can see !
They all are dancing in the crimson blaze.

Look how their garments wave, their jewels
    shine,
When the smoke parts a bit.   The tall flames
    dart.
Is not the fire real fire ?   They fear it not.

VOICES WITHOUT.

Arise, oh house of Jacob.   Let us walk
Within the light of the Almighty Lord !

Enter in furious haste PRINCE WILLIAM *and* NORDMANN.

PRINCE WILLIAM.

Respite !   You kill your daughter, Henry Schnet-
    zen !

NORDMANN.

Liebhaid von Orb is your own flesh and blood.

SCHNETZEN.

Spectre ! do dead men rise ?

NORDMANN.

                    Yea, for revenge !
I swear, Lord Schnetzen, by my knightly honor,
She who is dancing yonder to her death,
Is thy wife's child !

    [SCHNETZEN *and* PRINCE WILLIAM *make a rush
      forward towards the flames.   Music ceases; a
      sound of crashing boards is heard and a great
      cry —* HALLELUJAH !

PRINCE WILLIAM *and* SCHNETZEN.

Too late! too late!

CITIZENS.

All 's done!

PRINCE WILLIAM.

The fire! the fire!   Liebhaid, I come to thee.

[*He is about to spring forward, but is held back by guards.*

SCHNETZEN.

Oh cruel Christ!   Is there no bolt in heaven
For the child murderer?   Kill me, my friends!
        my breast
Is bare to all your swords.

[*He tears open his jerkin, and falls unconscious.*
[*Curtain falls.*

THE END.[1]

---

[1] The plot and incidents of this Tragedy are taken from a little narrative entitled " *Der Tanz zum Tode; ein Nachtstück aus dem vierzehnten Jahrhundert,*" (The Dance to Death — a Night-piece of the fourteenth century). By Richard Reinhard. Compiled from authentic documents communicated by Professor Franz Delitzsch.

The original narrative thus disposes, in conclusion, of the principal characters : —

" The Knight Henry Schnetzen ended his curse-stricken life in a cloister of the strictest order.

" Herr Nordmann was placed in close confinement, and during the same year his head fell under the sword of the executioner.

" Prince William returned, broken down with sorrow, to Eisenach. His princely father's heart found no comfort during the remainder of his days. He died soon after the murder of the Jews — his last words were, ' woe ! the fire ! '

"William reached an advanced age, but his life was joyless. He never married, and at his death Meissen was inherited by his nephew.

" The Jewish cemetery in Nordhausen, the scene of this martyrdom, lay for a long time waste. Nobody would build upon it. Now it is a bleaching meadow, and where once the flames sprang up, to-day rests peaceful sunshine."

TRANSLATIONS.

TRANSLATIONS

FROM THE HEBREW POETS OF MEDIÆVAL SPAIN.

SOLOMON BEN JUDAH GABIROL.

(DIED BETWEEN 1070–80.)

" Am I sipping the honey of the lips ?
Am I drunk with the wine of a kiss ?
Have I culled the flowers of the cheek,
Have I sucked the fresh fragrance of the breath ?
Nay, it is the Song of Gabirol that has revived me,
The perfume of his youthful, spring-tide breeze."
MOSES BEN ESRA.

" I will engrave my songs indelibly upon the heart of the world,
so that no one can efface them."   GABIROL.

NIGHT-PIECE.

NIGHT, and the heavens beam serene with peace,
Like a pure heart benignly smiles the moon.
Oh, guard thy blessed beauty from mischance,
This I beseech thee in all tender love.
See where the Storm his cloudy mantle spreads,
An ashy curtain covereth the moon.
As if the tempest thirsted for the rain,
The clouds he presses, till they burst in streams.

Heaven wears a dusky raiment, and the moon
Appeareth dead — her tomb is yonder cloud,
And weeping shades come after, like the people
Who mourn with tearful grief a noble queen.
But look ! the thunder pierced night's close-linked
      mail,
His keen-tipped lance of lightning brandishing;
He hovers like a seraph-conqueror. —
Dazed by the flaming splendor of his wings,
In rapid flight as in a whirling dance,
The black cloud-ravens hurry scared away.
So, though the powers of darkness chain my soul,
My heart, a hero, chafes and breaks its bonds.

NIGHT-THOUGHTS.

WILL night already spread her wings and weave
Her dusky robe about the day's bright form,
Boldly the sun's fair countenance displacing,
And swathe it with her shadow in broad day ?
So a green wreath of mist enrings the moon,
Till envious clouds do quite encompass her.
No wind ! and yet the slender stem is stirred,
With faint, slight motion as from inward tremor.
Mine eyes are full of grief — who sees me, asks,
"Oh wherefore dost thou cling unto the
      ground ?"
My friends discourse with sweet and soothing
      words ;
They all are vain, they glide above my head.

I fain would check my tears; would fain enlarge
Unto infinity, my heart — in vain!
Grief presses hard my breast, therefore my tears
Have scarcely dried, ere they again spring forth.
For these are streams no furnace heat may
      quench,
Nebuchadnezzar's flames may dry them not.
What is the pleasure of the day for me,
If, in its crucible, I must renew
Incessantly the pangs of purifying?
Up, challenge, wrestle, and o'ercome! Be
      strong!
The late grapes cover all the vine with fruit.
I am not glad, though even the lion's pride
Content itself upon the field's poor grass.
My spirit sinks beneath the tide, soars not
With fluttering seamews on the moist, soft strand.
I follow Fortune not, where'er she lead.
Lord o'er myself, I banish her, compel,
And though her clouds should rain no blessed
      dew,
Though she withhold the crown, the heart's de-
      sire,
Though all deceive, though honey change to gall,
Still am I lord, and will in freedom strive.

MEDITATIONS.

Forget thine anguish,
    Vexed heart, again.
Why shouldst thou languish,

    With earthly pain?
The husk shall slumber,
    Bedded in clay
Silent and sombre,
    Oblivion's prey!
But, Spirit immortal,
Thou at Death's portal,
    Tremblest with fear.
    If he caress thee,
    Curse thee or bless thee,
    Thou must draw near,
From him the worth of thy works to hear.

    Why full of terror,
    Compassed with error,
    Trouble thy heart,
    For thy mortal part?
    The soul flies home —
    The corpse is dumb.
    Of all thou didst have,
Follows naught to the grave.
    Thou fliest thy nest,
Swift as a bird to thy place of rest.

    What avail grief and fasting,
    Where nothing is lasting?
    Pomp, domination,
    Become tribulation.
    In a health-giving draught,
    A death-dealing shaft.

Wealth — an illusion,
Power — a lie,
Over all, dissolution
Creeps silent and sly.
Unto others remain
The goods thou didst gain
With infinite pain.

Life is a vine-branch;
A vintager, Death.
He threatens and lowers
More near with each breath.
Then hasten, arise !
Seek God, O my soul !
For time quickly flies,
Still far is the goal.
Vain heart praying dumbly,
Learn to prize humbly,
The meanest of fare.
Forget all thy sorrow,
Behold, Death is there !

Dove-like lamenting,
Be full of repenting,
Lift vision supernal
To raptures eternal.
On ev'ry occasion
Seek lasting salvation.
Pour thy heart out in weeping,
While others are sleeping.

Pray to Him when all 's still,
Performing his will.
And so shall the angel of peace be thy warden,
And guide thee at last to the heavenly garden.

HYMN.

ALMIGHTY ! what is man ?
But flesh and blood.
Like shadows flee his days,
He marks not how they vanish from his gaze,
Suddenly, he must die —
He droppeth, stunned, into nonentity.

Almighty ! what is man ?
A body frail and weak,
Full of deceit and lies,
Of vile hypocrisies.
Now like a flower blowing,
Now scorched by sunbeams glowing.
And wilt thou of his trespasses inquire ?
How may he ever bear
Thine anger just, thy vengeance dire ?
Punish him not, but spare,
For he is void of power and strength !

Almighty ! what is man ?
By filthy lust possessed,
Whirled in a round of lies,
Fond frenzy swells his breast.
The pure man sinks in mire and slime,

The noble shrinketh not from crime,
Wilt thou resent on him the charms of sin?
  Like fading grass,
  So shall he pass.
  Like chaff that blows
  Where the wind goes.
Then spare him, be thou merciful, O King,
Upon the dreaded day of reckoning!

  Almighty! what is man?
    The haughty son of time
  Drinks deep of sin,
    And feeds on crime
Seething like waves that roll,
Hot as a glowing coal.
And wilt thou punish him for sins inborn?
  Lost and forlorn,
Then like the weakling he must fall,
Who some great hero strives withal.
Oh, spare him, therefore! let him win
  Grace for his sin!

  Almighty! what is man?
    Spotted in guilty wise,
  A stranger unto faith,
    Whose tongue is stained with lies,
And shalt thou count his sins — so is he lost,
  Uprooted by thy breath.
Like to a stream by tempest tossed,
His life falls from him like a cloak,

He passes into nothingness, like smoke.
  Then spare him, punish not, be kind, I pray,
To him who dwelleth in the dust, an image
        wrought in clay!

      Almighty! what is man?
          A withered bough!
When he is awe-struck by approaching doom,
Like a dried blade of grass, so weak, so low
The pleasure of his life is changed to gloom.
He crumbles like a garment spoiled with moth;
According to his sins wilt thou be wroth?
He melts like wax before the candle's breath,
Yea, like thin water, so he vanisheth,
Oh, spare him therefore, for thy gracious name,
And be not too severe upon his shame!

      Almighty! what is man?
          A faded leaf!
If thou dost weigh him in the balance — lo!
He disappears — a breath that thou dost blow.
      His heart is ever filled
      With lust of lies unstilled.
      Wilt thou bear in mind his crime
      Unto all time?
He fades away like clouds sun-kissed,
      Dissolves like mist.
Then spare him! let him love and mercy win,
According to thy grace, and not according to his
        sin!

TO A DETRACTOR.

THE Autumn promised, and he keeps
His word unto the meadow-rose.
The pure, bright lightnings herald Spring,
Serene and glad the fresh earth shows.
The rain has quenched her children's thirst,
Her cheeks, but now so cold and dry,
Are soft and fair, a laughing face ;
With clouds of purple shines the sky,
Though filled with light, yet veiled with haze.
Hark ! hark ! the turtle's mocking note
Outsings the valley-pigeon's lays.
Her wings are gemmed, and from her throat,
When the clear sun gleams back again,
It seems to me as though she wore
About her neck a jewelled chain.
Say, wilt thou darken such a light,
Wilt drag the clouds from heaven's height ?
Although thy heart with anger swell,
Yet firm as marble mine doth dwell.
Therein no fear thy wrath begets.
It is not shaken by thy threats.
Yea, hurl thy darts, thy weapons wield,
The strength of youth is still my shield.
My winged steed toward the heights doth bound,
The dust whirls upward from the ground ;
My song is scanty, dost thou deem
Thine eloquence a mighty stream ?
Only the blameless offering.

Not the profusion man may bring,
Prevaileth with our Lord and King.
The long days out of minutes grow,
And out of months the years arise,
Wilt thou be master of the wise,
Then learn the hidden stream to know,
That from the inmost heart doth flow.

FRAGMENT.

MY friend spoke with insinuating tongue :
"Drink wine, and thy flesh shall be made
whole. Look how it hisses in the leathern
bottle like a captured serpent."
Oh fool! can the sun be forged into a cask
stopped with earthly bungs. I know not that
the power of wine has ever overmastered my
sorrows; for these mighty giants I have found
as yet no resting-place.

STANZAS.

"WITH tears thy grief thou dost bemoan,
Tears that would melt the hardest stone,
Oh, wherefore sing'st thou not the vine?
Why chant'st thou not the praise of wine?
It chases pain with cunning art,
The craven slinks from out thy heart."

But I: Poor fools the wine may cheat,
Lull them with lying visions sweet.
Upon the wings of storms may bear

The heavy burden of their care.
The father's heart may harden so,
He feeleth not his own child's woe.

No ocean is the cup, no sea,
To drown my broad, deep misery.
It grows so rank, you cut it all,
The aftermath springs just as tall.
My heart and flesh are worn away,
Mine eyes are darkened from the day.

The lovely morning-red behold
Wave to the breeze her flag of gold.
The hosts of stars above the world,
Like banners vanishing are furled.
The dew shines bright; I bide forlorn,
And shudder with the chill of morn.

WINE AND GRIEF.

WITH heavy groans did I approach my friends,
Heavy as though the mountains I would move.
The flagon they were murdering; they poured
Into the cup, wild-eyed, the grape's red blood.
No, they killed not, they breathed new life
 therein.
Then, too, in fiery rapture, burned my veins,
But soon the fumes had fled. In vain, in vain!
Ye cannot fill the breach of the rent heart.
Ye crave a sensuous joy; ye strive in vain
To cheat with flames of passion, my despair.

So when the sinking sun draws near to night,
The sky's bright cheeks fade 'neath those tresses
  black.
Ye laugh — but silently the soul weeps on;
Ye cannot stifle her sincere lament.

DEFIANCE.

" CONQUER the gloomy night of thy sorrow, for
  the morning greets thee with laughter.
Rise and clothe thyself with noble pride,
Break loose from the tyranny of grief.
Thou standest alone among men,
Thy song is like a pearl in beauty."

So spake my friend.   'T is well!
The billows of the stormy sea which overwhelmed
  my soul, —
These I subdue ; I quake not
Before the bow and arrow of destiny.
I endured with patience when he deceitfully lied
  to me
With his treacherous smile.

Yea, boldly I defy Fate,
I cringe not to envious Fortune.
I mock the towering floods.
My brave heart does not shrink —
This heart of mine, that, albeit young in years,
Is none the less rich in deep, keen-eyed expe-
  rience.

A DEGENERATE AGE.

WHERE is the man who has been tried and found
    strong and sound ?
Where is the friend of reason and of knowledge ?
I see only sceptics and weaklings.
I see only prisoners in the durance of the senses.
And every fool and every spendthrift
Thinks himself as great a master as Aristotle.
Think'st thou that they have written poems ?
Call'st thou that a Song ?
I call it the cackling of ravens.
The zeal of the prophet must free poesy
From the embrace of wanton youths.
My song I have inscribed on the forehead of
    Time,
They know and hate it — for it is lofty.

ABUL HASSAN JUDAH BEN HA-LEVI.

(BORN BETWEEN 1080-90.)

A LETTER TO HIS FRIEND ISAAC.

BUT yesterday the earth drank like a child
    With eager thirst the autumn rain.
Or like a wistful bride who waits the hour
    Of love's mysterious bliss and pain.
And now the Spring is here with yearning eyes ;
    Midst shimmering golden flower-beds,
On meadows carpeted with varied hues,
    In richest raiment clad, she treads.
She weaves a tapestry of bloom o'er all,
    And myriad eyed young plants upspring,
White, green, or red like lips that to the mouth
    Of the beloved one sweetly cling.
Whence come these radiant tints, these blended
      beams ?
    Here 's such a dazzle, such a blaze,
As though earth stole the splendor of the stars,
    Fain to eclipse them with her rays.
Come ! go we to the garden with our wine,
    Which scatters sparks of hot desire,
Within our hand 't is cold, but in our veins
    It flashes clear, it glows like fire.
It bubbles sunnily in earthen jugs.
We catch it in the crystal glass,

Then wander through cool, shadowy lanes and
  breathe
The spicy freshness of the grass.
Whilst we with happy hearts our circuit keep,
 The gladness of the Earth is shown.
She smileth, though the trickling rain-drops
  weep
 Silently o'er her, one by one.
She loves to feel the tears upon her cheek,
 Like a rich veil, with pearls inwove.
Joyous she listens when the swallows chirp,
 And warbles to her mate, the dove.
Blithe as a maiden midst the young green leaves,
 A wreath she 'll wind, a fragrant treasure ;
All living things in graceful motion leap,
 As dancing to some merry measure.
The morning breezes rustle cordially,
 Love's thirst is sated with the balm they send.
Sweet breathes the myrtle in the frolic wind,
 As though remembering a distant friend.
The myrtle branch now proudly lifted high,
 Now whispering to itself drops low again.
The topmost palm-leaves rapturously stir,
 For all at once they hear the birds' soft strain.
So stirs, so yearns all nature, gayly decked,
 To honor *Isaac* with her best array.
Hear'st thou the word ? She cries — I beam
  with joy,
Because with Isaac I am wed to-day.

ADMONITION.

Long in the lap of childhood didst thou sleep,
Think how thy youth like chaff did disappear ;
Shall life's sweet Spring forever last ?   Look up,
Old age approaches ominously near.
Oh shake thou off the world, even as the bird
Shakes off the midnight dew that clogged his
      wings.
Soar upward, seek redemption from thy guilt
And from the earthly dross that round thee
      clings.
Draw near to God, His holy angels know,
For whom His bounteous streams of mercy flow.

LOVE-SONG.

" See'st thou o'er my shoulders falling,
    Snake-like ringlets waving free ?
Have no fear, for they are twisted
    To allure thee unto me."

Thus she spake, the gentle dove,
    Listen to thy plighted love : —
" Ah, how long I wait, until
    Sweetheart cometh back (she said)
Laying his caressing hand
    Underneath my burning head."

SEPARATION.

AND so we twain must part! Oh linger yet,
  Let me still feed my glance upon thine eyes.
Forget not, love, the days of our delight,
  And I our nights of bliss shall ever prize.
In dreams thy shadowy image I shall see,
  Oh even in my dream be kind to me!

Though I were dead, I none the less would
    hear
  Thy step, thy garment rustling on the sand.
And if thou waft me greetings from the grave,
  I shall drink deep the breath of that cold
    land.
Take thou my days, command this life of mine,
  If it can lengthen out the space of thine.

No voice I hear from lips death-pale and chill,
  Yet deep within my heart it echoes still.
My frame remains — my soul to thee yearns
    forth.
  A shadow I must tarry still on earth.
Back to the body dwelling here in pain,
  Return, my soul, make haste and come again!

LONGING FOR JERUSALEM.

O CITY of the world, with sacred splendor blest,
My spirit yearns to thee from out the far-off
    West,

A stream of love wells forth when I recall thy
 day,
Now is thy temple waste, thy glory passed away.
Had I an eagle's wings, straight would I fly to
 thee,
Moisten thy holy dust with wet cheeks stream-
 ing free.
Oh, how I long for thee! albeit thy King has
 gone,
Albeit where balm once flowed, the serpent
 dwells alone.
Could I but kiss thy dust, so would I fain
 expire,
As sweet as honey then, my passion, my desire!

ON THE VOYAGE TO JERUSALEM.

I.

My two-score years and ten are over,
 Never again shall youth be mine.
The years are ready-winged for flying,
 What crav'st thou still of feast and wine?
Wilt thou still court man's acclamation,
 Forgetting what the Lord hath said?
And forfeiting thy weal eternal,
 By thine own guilty heart misled?
Shalt thou have never done with folly,
 Still fresh and new must it arise?
Oh heed it not, heed not the senses,
 But follow God, be meek and wise;

Yea, profit by thy days remaining,
   They hurry swiftly to the goal.
Be zealous in the Lord's high service,
   And banish falsehood from thy soul.
Use all thy strength, use all thy fervor,
   Defy thine own desires, awaken!
Be not afraid when seas are foaming,
   And earth to her foundations shaken.
Benumbed the hand then of the sailor,
   The captain's skill and power are lamed.
Gayly they sailed with colors flying,
   And now turn home again ashamed.
The ocean is our only refuge,
   The sandbank is our only goal,
The masts are swaying as with terror,
   And quivering does the vessel roll.
The mad wind frolics with the billows,
   Now smooths them low, now lashes high.
Now they are storming up like lions,
   And now like serpents sleek they lie;
And wave on wave is ever pressing,
   They hiss, they whisper, soft of tone.
Alack! was that the vessel splitting?
   Are sail and mast and rudder gone?
Here, screams of fright, there, silent weeping,
   The bravest feels his courage fail.
What stead our prudence or our wisdom?
   The soul itself can naught avail.
And each one to his God is crying,
   Soar up, my soul, to Him aspire,

Who wrought a miracle for Jordan,
    Extol Him, oh angelic choir!
Remember Him who stays the tempest,
    The stormy billows doth control,
Who quickeneth the lifeless body,
    And fills the empty frame with soul.
Behold! once more appears a wonder,
    The angry waves erst raging wild,
Like quiet flocks of sheep reposing,
    So soft, so still, so gently mild.
The sun descends, and high in heaven,
    The golden-circled moon doth stand.
Within the sea the stars are straying,
    Like wanderers in an unknown land.
The lights celestial in the waters
    Are flaming clearly as above,
As though the very heavens descended,
    To seal a covenant of love.
Perchance both sea and sky, twin oceans,
    From the same source of grace are sprung.
'Twixt these my heart, a third sea, surges,
    With songs resounding, clearly sung.

II.

A watery waste the sinful world has grown,
With no dry spot whereon the eye can rest,
No man, no beast, no bird to gaze upon,
Can all be dead, with silent sleep possessed?
Oh, how I long the hills and vales to see,
To find myself on barren steppes were bliss.

I peer about, but nothing greeteth me,
Naught save the ship, the clouds, the waves'
     abyss,
The crocodile which rushes from the deeps;
The flood foams gray; the whirling waters reel,
Now like its prey whereon at last it sweeps,
The ocean swallows up the vessel's keel.
The billows rage — exult, oh soul of mine,
Soon shalt thou enter the Lord's sacred shrine!

III.

TO THE WEST WIND.

O WEST, how fragrant breathes thy gentle air,
Spikenard and aloes on thy pinions glide.
Thou blow'st from spicy chambers, not from there
Where angry winds and tempests fierce abide.
As on a bird's wings thou dost waft me home,
Sweet as a bundle of rich myrrh to me.
And after thee yearn all the throngs that roam
And furrow with light keel the rolling sea.
Desert her not — our ship — bide with her oft,
When the day sinks and in the morning light.
Smooth thou the deeps and make the billows soft,
Nor rest save at our goal, the sacred height.
Chide thou the East that chafes the raging flood,
And swells the towering surges wild and rude.
What can I do, the elements' poor slave?
Now do they hold me fast, now leave me free;
Cling to the Lord, my soul, for He will save,
Who caused the mountains and the winds to be.

MOSES BEN ESRA.

(ABOUT 1100.)

EXTRACTS FROM THE BOOK OF TARSHISH, OR "NECKLACE OF PEARLS."

I.

THE shadow of the houses leave behind,
In the cool boscage of the grove reclined,
The wine of friendship from love's goblet drink,
And entertain with cheerful speech the mind.

Drink, friend! behold, the dreary winter's
      gone,
The mantle of old age has time withdrawn.
The sunbeam glitters in the morning dew,
O'er hill and vale youth's bloom is surging on.

Cup-bearer! quench with snow the goblet's fire,
Even as the wise man cools and stills his ire.
Look, when the jar is drained, upon the brim
The light foam melteth with the heart's desire.

Cup-bearer! bring anear the silver bowl,
And with the glowing gold fulfil the whole,
Unto the weak new vigor it imparts,
And without lance subdues the hero's soul.

My love sways, dancing, like the myrtle-tree,
The masses of her curls disheveled, see !
She kills me with her darts, intoxicates
My burning blood, and will not set me free.

Within the aromatic garden come,
And slowly in its shadows let us roam,
The foliage be the turban for our brows,
And the green branches o'er our heads a dome.

All pain thou with the goblet shalt assuage,
The wine-cup heals the sharpest pangs that rage,
Let others crave inheritance of wealth,
Joy be our portion and our heritage.

Drink in the garden, friend, anigh the rose,
Richer than spice's breath the soft air blows.
If it should cease a little traitor then,
A zephyr light its secret would disclose.

II.

Thou who art clothed in silk, who drawest on
Proudly thy raiment of fine linen spun,
Bethink thee of the day when thou alone
Shalt dwell at last beneath the marble stone.

Anigh the nests of adders thine abode,
With the earth-crawling serpent and the toad.
Trust in the Lord, He will sustain thee there,
And without fear thy soul shall rest with God.

If the world flatter thee with soft-voiced art,
Know 't is a cunning witch who charms thy heart,
Whose habit is to wed man's soul with grief,
And those who are close-bound in love to part.

He who bestows his wealth upon the poor,
Has only lent it to the Lord, be sure —
Of what avail to clasp it with clenched hand?
It goes not with us to the grave obscure.

The voice of those who dwell within the tomb,
Who in corruption's house have made their home;
"O ye who wander o'er us still to-day,
When will ye come to share with us the gloom?"

How can'st thou ever of the world complain,
And murmuring, burden it with all thy pain?
Silence! thou art a traveller at an inn,
A guest, who may but over night remain.

Be thou not wroth against the proud, but show
How he who yesterday great joy did know,
To-day is begging for his very bread,
And painfully upon a crutch must go.

How foolish they whose faith is fixed upon
The treasures of their worldly wealth alone,
Far wiser were it to obey the Lord,
And only say, " The will of God be done ! "

Has Fortune smiled on thee ?   Oh do not trust
Her reckless joy, she still deceives and must.
Perpetual snares she spreads about thy feet,
Thou shalt not rest till thou art mixed with dust.

Man is a weaver on the earth, 't is said,
Who weaves and weaves — his own days are the
       thread,
And when the length allotted he hath spun,
All life is over, and all hope is dead.

IN THE NIGHT.

UNTO the house of prayer my spirit yearns,
Unto the sources of her being turns,
To where the sacred light of heaven burns,
She struggles thitherward by day and night.

The splendor of God's glory blinds her eyes,
Up without wings she soareth to the skies,
With silent aspiration seeks to rise,
In dusky evening and in darksome night.

To her the wonders of God's works appear,
She longs with fervor Him to draw anear,
The tidings of His glory reach her ear,
From morn to even, and from night to night.

The banner of thy grace did o'er me rest,
Yet was thy worship banished from my breast.

Almighty, thou didst seek me out and test
To try and to instruct me in the night.

I dare not idly on my pillow lie,
With winged feet to the shrine I fain would fly,
When chained by leaden slumbers heavily,
Men rest in imaged shadows, dreams of night.

Infatuate I trifled youth away,
In nothingness dreamed through my manhood's
     day.
Therefore my streaming tears I may not stay,
They are my meat and drink by day and night.

In flesh imprisoned is the son of light,
This life is but a bridge when seen aright.
Rise in the silent hour and pray with might,
Awake and call upon thy God by night!

Hasten to cleanse thyself of sin, arise!
Follow Truth's path that leads unto the skies,
As swift as yesterday existence flies,
Brief even as a watch within the night.

Man enters life for trouble; all he has,
And all that he beholds, is pain, alas!
Like to a flower does he bloom and pass,
He fadeth like a vision of the night.

The surging floods of life around him roar,
Death feeds upon him, pity is no more,

To others all his riches he gives o'er,
And dieth in the middle hour of night.

Crushed by the burden of my sins I pray,
Oh, wherefore shunned I not the evil way?
Deep are my sighs, I weep the livelong day,
And wet my couch with tears night after night.

My spirit stirs, my streaming tears still run,
Like to the wild birds' notes my sorrows' tone,
In the hushed silence loud resounds my groan,
My soul arises moaning in the night.

Within her narrow cell oppressed with dread,
Bare of adornment and with grief-bowed head
Lamenting, many a tear her sad eyes shed,
She weeps with anguish in the gloomy night.

For tears my burden seem to lighten best,
Could I but weep my heart's blood, I might rest.
My spirit bows with mighty grief oppressed,
I utter forth my prayer within the night.

Youth's charm has like a fleeting shadow gone,
With eagle wings the hours of life have flown.
Alas! the time when pleasure I have known,
I may not now recall by day or night.

The haughty scorn pursues me of my foe,
Evil his thought, yet soft his speech and low.

Forget it not, but bear his purpose so
Forever in thy mind by day and night.

Observe a pious fast, be whole again,
Hasten to purge thy heart of every stain.
No more from prayer and penitence refrain,
But turn unto thy God by day and night.

He speaks: "My son, yea, I will send thee aid,
Bend thou thy steps to me, be not afraid.
No nearer friend than I am, hast thou made,
Possess thy soul in patience one more night."

FROM THE "DIVAN."

MY thoughts impelled me to the resting-place
Where sleep my parents, many a friend and
      brother.
I asked them (no one heard and none replied):
"Do ye forsake me, too, oh father, mother?"
Then from the grave, without a tongue, these
      cried,
And showed my own place waiting by their side.

LOVE SONG OF ALCHARISI.

I.

THE long-closed door, oh open it again, send me
      back once more my fawn that had fled.
On the day of our reunion, thou shalt rest by my
      side, there wilt thou shed over me the
      streams of thy delicious perfume.

Oh beautiful bride, what is the form of thy
 friend, that thou say to me, Release him,
 send him away?

He is the beautiful-eyed one of ruddy glorious
 aspect — that is my friend, him do thou
 detain.

II.

Hail to thee, Son of my friend, the ruddy, the
 bright-colored one! Hail to thee whose
 temples are like a pomegranate.

Hasten to the refuge of thy sister, and protect
 the son of Isaiah against the troops of the
 Ammonites.

What art thou, O Beauty, that thou shouldst in-
 spire love? that thy voice should ring like
 the voices of the bells upon the priestly
 garments?

The hour wherein thou desireth my love, I shall
 hasten to meet thee. Softly will I drop
 beside thee like the dew upon Hermon.

NACHUM.

SPRING SONGS.

I.

Now the dreary winter's over,
 Fled with him are grief and pain,
When the trees their bloom recover,
 Then the soul is born again.

Spikenard blossoms shaking,
  Perfume all the air,
And in bud and flower breaking,
  Stands my garden fair.
While with swelling gladness blest,
Heaves my friend's rejoicing breast.
Oh, come home, lost friend of mine,
Scared from out my tent and land.
  Drink from me the spicy wine,
  Milk and must from out my hand.

Cares which hovered round my brow,
Vanish, while the garden now
Girds itself with myrtle hedges,
          Bright-hued edges
          Round it lie.
          Suddenly
All my sorrows die.
See the breathing myrrh-trees blow,
  Aromatic airs enfold me.
While the splendor and the glow
  Of the walnut-branches hold me.

And a balsam-breath is flowing,
  Through the leafy shadows green,
On the left the cassia 's growing,
  On the right the aloe 's seen.
Lo, the clear cup crystalline,
  In itself a gem of art,
Ruby-red foams up with wine,

Sparkling rich with froth and bubble.
I forget the want and trouble,
  Buried deep within my heart.

Where is he who lingered here,
 But a little while agone?
From my homestead he has flown,
From the city sped alone,
Dwelling in the forest drear.
Oh come again, to those who wait thee long,
And who will greet thee with a choral song!
  Beloved, kindle bright
Once more thine everlasting light.
Through thee, oh cherub with protecting wings,
My glory out of darkness springs.

II.

Crocus and spikenard blossom on my lawn,
The brier fades, the thistle is withdrawn.
Behold, where glass-clear brooks are flowing,
The splendor of the myrtle blowing!
The garden-tree has doffed her widow's veil,
And shines in festal garb, in verdure pale.
  The turtle-dove is cooing, hark!
 Is that the warble of the lark!
Unto their perches they return again.
Oh brothers, carol forth your joyous strain,
Pour out full-throated ecstasy of mirth,
Proclaiming the Lord's glory to the earth.

One with a low, sweet song,
One echoing loud and long,
Chanting the music of a spirit strong.

In varied tints the landscape glows.
In rich array appears the rose.
While the pomegranate's wreath of green,
The gauzy red and snow-white blossoms screen.
Who loves it, now rejoices for its sake,
And those are glad who sleep, and those who
wake.
When cool-breathed evening visiteth the world,
In flower and leaf the beaded dew is pearled,
Reviving all that droops at length,
And to the languid giving strength.

Now in the east the shining light behold!
The sun has oped a lustrous path of gold.
Within my narrow garden's greenery,
Shot forth a branch, sprang to a splendid tree,
Then in mine ear the joyous words did ring,
"From Jesse's root a verdant branch shall
spring."
My Friend has cast His eyes upon my grief,
According to His mercy, sends relief.
Hark! the redemption hour's resounding stroke,
For him who bore with patient heart the yoke!

A TRANSLATION AND TWO IMITA-TIONS.

I.

DONNA CLARA.

(FROM THE GERMAN OF HEINE.)

In the evening through her garden
　　Wanders the Alcalde's daughter,
Festal sounds of drum and trumpet
　　Ring out hither from the Castle.

"I am weary of the dances,
　　Honeyed words of adulation
From the knights who still compare me
　　To the sun with dainty phrases.

"Yes, of all things I am weary,
　　Since I first beheld by moonlight
Him, my cavalier, whose zither
　　Nightly draws me to my casement.

"As he stands so slim and daring,
　　With his flaming eyes that sparkle,
And with nobly pallid features,
　　Truly, he St. George resembles."

Thus went Donna Clara dreaming,
 On the ground her eyes were fastened.
When she raised them, lo! before her
 Stood the handsome knightly stranger.

Pressing hands and whispering passion,
 These twain wander in the moonlight,
Gently doth the breeze caress them,
 The enchanted roses greet them.

The enchanted roses greet them,
 And they glow like Love's own heralds.
"Tell me, tell me, my beloved,
 Wherefore all at once thou blushest?"

"Gnats were stinging me, my darling,
 And I hate these gnats in summer
E'en as though they were a rabble
 Of vile Jews with long, hooked noses."

"Heed not gnats nor Jews, beloved,"
 Spake the knight with fond endearments.
From the almond-trees dropped downward
 Myriad snowy flakes of blossoms.

Myriad snowy flakes of blossoms
 Shed around them fragrant odors.
"Tell me, tell me, my beloved,
 Looks thy heart on me with favor?"

" Yes, I love thee, O my darling,
    And I swear it by our Saviour,
  Whom the accursed Jews did murder,
    Long ago with wicked malice."

" Heed thou neither Jews nor Saviour,"
    Spake the knight with fond endearments.
  Far off waved, as in a vision,
    Gleaming lilies bathed in moonlight.

  Gleaming lilies bathed in moonlight
    Seemed to watch the stars above them.
" Tell me, tell me, my beloved,
    Didst thou not erewhile swear falsely ? "

" Naught is false in me, my darling,
    E'en as in my veins there floweth
  Not a drop of blood that 's Moorish,
    Neither of foul Jewish current."

" Heed not Moors nor Jews, beloved,"
    Spake the knight with fond endearments.
  Then towards a grove of myrtles
    Leads he the Alcalde's daughter.

  And with Love's slight subtile meshes,
    He has trapped her and entangled.
  Brief their words, but long their kisses,
    For their hearts are overflowing.

What a melting bridal carol
  Sings the nightingale, the pure one.
How the fire-flies in the grasses
  Trip their sparkling torchlight dances!

In the grove the silence deepens,
  Naught is heard save furtive rustling
Of the swaying myrtle branches,
  And the breathing of the flowers.

But the sound of drum and trumpet
  Burst forth sudden from the castle.
Rudely they awaken Clara,
  Pillowed on her lover's bosom.

"Hark! they summon me, my darling!
  But before we part, oh tell me,
Tell me what thy precious name is,
  Which so closely thou hast hidden."

Then the knight with gentle laughter,
  Kissed the fingers of his Donna,
Kissed her lips and kissed her forehead,
  And at last these words he uttered:

"I, Señora, your beloved,
  Am the son of the respected,
Worthy, erudite Grand Rabbi,
  Israel of Saragossa."

The *ensemble* of the romance is a scene of my own life — only the Park of Berlin has become the Alcalde's garden, the Baroness a Señora, and myself a St. George, or even an Apollo. This was only to be the first part of a trilogy, the second of which shows the hero jeered at by his own child, who does not know him, whilst the third discovers this child, who has become a Dominican, and is torturing to the death his Jewish brethren. The refrain of these two pieces corresponds with that of the first. Indeed this little poem was not intended to excite laughter, still less to denote a mocking spirit. I merely wished, without any definite purpose, to render with epic impartiality in this poem an individual circumstance, and, at the same time, something general and universal — a moment in the world's history which was distinctly reflected in my experience, and I had conceived the whole idea in a spirit which was anything rather than smiling, but serious and painful, so much so, that it was to form the first part of a tragic trilogy. — *Heine's Correspondence.*

Guided by these hints, I have endeavored to carry out in the two following original Ballads the Poet's first conception.

Emma Lazarus.

II.

DON PEDRILLO.

Not a lad in Saragossa
   Nobler-featured, haughtier-tempered,
Than the Alcalde's youthful grandson,
   Donna Clara's boy Pedrillo.

Handsome as the Prince of Evil,
   And devout as St. Ignatius.

Deft at fence, unmatched with zither,
    Miniature of knightly virtues.

Truly an unfailing blessing
    To his pious, widowed mother,
To the beautiful, lone matron
    Who forswore the world to rear him.

For her beauty hath but ripened
    In such wise as the pomegranate
Putteth by her crown of blossoms,
    For her richer crown of fruitage.

Still her hand is claimed and courted,
    Still she spurns her proudest suitors,
Doting on a phantom passion,
    And upon her boy Pedrillo.

Like a saint lives Donna Clara,
    First at matins, last at vespers,
Half her fortune she expendeth
    Buying masses for the needy.

Visiting the poor afflicted,
    Infinite is her compassion,
Scorning not the Moorish beggar,
    Nor the wretched Jew despising.

And — a scandal to the faithful,
    E'en she hath been known to welcome

To her castle the young Rabbi,
   Offering to his tribe her bounty.

Rarely hath he crossed the threshold,
   Yet the thought that he hath crossed it,
Burns like poison in the marrow
   Of the zealous youth Pedrillo.

By the blessed Saint Iago,
   He hath vowed immortal hatred
To these circumcised intruders
   Who pollute the soil of Spaniards.

Seated in his mother's garden,
   At high noon the boy Pedrillo
Playeth with his favorite parrot,
   Golden-green with streaks of scarlet.

" Pretty Dodo, speak thy lesson,"
   Coaxed Pedrillo — " thief and traitor " —
" Thief and traitor " — croaked the parrot,
  " Is the yellow-skirted Rabbi."

And the boy with peals of laughter,
   Stroked his favorite's head of emerald,
Raised his eyes, and lo ! before him
   Stood the yellow-skirted Rabbi.

In his dark eyes gleamed no anger,
   No hot flush o'erspread his features.

'Neath his beard his pale lips quivered,
    And a shadow crossed his forehead.

Very gentle was his aspect,
    And his voice was mild and friendly,
" Evil words, my son, thou speakest,
    Teaching to the fowls of heaven.

" In our Talmud it stands written,
    Thrice curst is the tongue of slander,
Poisoning also with its victim,
    Him who speaks and him who listens."

But no whit abashed, Pedrillo,
    " What care I for curse of Talmud?
'T is no slander to speak evil
    Of the murderers of our Saviour.

" To your beard I will repeat it,
    That I only bide my manhood,
To wreak all my lawful hatred,
    On thyself and on thy people."

Very gently spoke the Rabbi,
    " Have a care, my son Pedrillo,
Thou art orphaned, and who knoweth
    But thy father loved this people?"

" Think you words like these will touch me?
    Such I laugh to scorn, sir Rabbi,

From high heaven, my sainted father
    On my deeds will smile in blessing.

" Loyal knight was he and noble,
    And my mother oft assures me,
Ne'er she saw so pure a Christian,
    'T is from him my zeal deriveth."

" What if he were such another
    As myself who stand before thee ? "
" I should curse the hour that bore me,
    I should die of shame and horror."

   " Harsher is thy creed than ours ;
    For had I a son as comely
As Pedrillo, I would love him,
    Love him were he thrice a Christian.

" In his youth my youth renewing
    Pamper, fondle, die to serve him,
Only breathing through his spirit —
    Couldst thou not love such a father ? "

Faltering spoke the deep-voiced Rabbi,
    With white lips and twitching fingers,
Then in clear, young, steady treble,
    Answered him the boy Pedrillo :

" At the thought my heart revolteth,
    All your tribe offend my senses,

They 're an eyesore to my vision,
   And a stench unto my nostrils.

" When I meet these unbelievers,
   With thick lips and eagle noses,
Thus I scorn them, thus revile them,
   Thus I spit upon their garment."

And the haughty youth passed onward,
   Bearing on his wrist his parrot,
And the yellow-skirted Rabbi
   With bowed head sought Donna Clara.

III

FRA PEDRO.

Golden lights and lengthening shadows,
   Flings the splendid sun declining,
O'er the monastery garden
   Rich in flower, fruit and foliage.

Through the avenue of nut trees,
   Pace two grave and ghostly friars,
Snowy white their gowns and girdles,
   Black as night their cowls and mantles.

Lithe and ferret-eyed the younger,
   Black his scapular denoting
A lay brother; his companion
   Large, imperious, towers above him.

'T is the abbot, great Fra Pedro,
   Famous through all Saragossa
For his quenchless zeal in crushing
   Heresy amidst his townfolk.

Handsome still with hood and tonsure,
   E'en as when the boy Pedrillo,
Insolent with youth and beauty,
   Who reviled the gentle Rabbi.

Lo, the level sun strikes sparkles
   From his dark eyes brightly flashing.
Stern his voice : " These too shall perish.
   I have vowed extermination.

" Tell not me of skill or virtue,
   Filial love or woman's beauty.
Jews are Jews, as serpents serpents,
   In themselves abomination."

Earnestly the other pleaded,
   " If my zeal, thrice reverend master,
E'er afforded thee assistance,
   Serving thee as flesh serves spirit,

" Hounding, scourging, flaying, burning,
   Casting into chains or exile,
At thy bidding these vile wretches,
   Hear and heed me now, my master.

" These be nowise like their brethren,
 Ben Jehudah is accounted
Saragossa's first physician,
 Loved by colleague as by patient.

" And his daughter Donna Zara
 Is our city's pearl of beauty,
Like the clusters of the vineyard
 Droop the ringlets o'er her temples.

" Like the moon in starry heavens
 Shines her face among her people,
And her form hath all the languor,
 Grace and glamour of the palm-tree.

" Well thou knowest, thrice reverend master,
 This is not their first affliction,
Was it not our Holy Office
 Whose bribed menials fired their dwelling?

" Ere dawn broke, the smoke ascended,
 Choked the stairways, filled the chambers,
Waked the household to the terror
 Of the flaming death that threatened.

" Then the poor bed-ridden mother
 Knew her hour had come ; two daughters,
Twinned in form, and mind, and spirit,
 And their father — who would save them?

"Towards her door sprang Ben Jehudah,
　　Donna Zara flew behind him
Round his neck her white arms wreathing,
　　Drew him from the burning chamber.

"There within, her sister Zillah
　　Stirred no limb to shun her torture,
Held her mother's hand and kissed her,
　　Saying, 'We will go together.'

"This the outer throng could witness,
　　As the flames enwound the dwelling,
Like a glory they illumined
　　Awfully the martyred daughter.

"Closer, fiercer, round they gathered,
　　Not a natural cry escaped her,
Helpless clung to her her mother,
　　Hand in hand they went together.

"Since that 'Act of Faith' three winters
　　Have rolled by, yet on the forehead
Of Jehudah is imprinted
　　Still the horror of that morning.

"Saragossa hath respected
　　His false creed; a man of sorrows,
He hath walked secure among us,
　　And his art repays our sufferance."

Thus he spoke and ceased.   The Abbot
  Lent him an impatient hearing,
Then outbroke with angry accent,
  " We have borne three years, thou sayest?

" 'T is enough ; my vow is sacred.
  These shall perish with their brethren.
Hark ye !   In my veins' pure current
  Were a single drop found Jewish,

"I would shrink not from outpouring
  All my life blood, but to purge it.
Shall I gentler prove to others ?
  Mercy would be sacrilegious.

"Ne'er again at thy soul's peril,
  Speak to me of Jewish beauty,
Jewish skill, or Jewish virtue.
  I have said.   Do thou remember."

Down behind the purple hillside
  Dropped the sun ; above the garden
Rang the Angelus' clear cadence
  Summoning the monks to vespers.

TRANSLATIONS FROM PETRARCH.

IN VITA. LXVII.

Since thou and I have proven many a time
That all our hope betrays us and deceives,
To that consummate good which never grieves
Uplift thy heart, towards a happier clime.
This life is like a field of flowering thyme,
Amidst the herbs and grass the serpent lives;
If aught unto the sight brief pleasure gives,
'T is but to snare the soul with treacherous lime.
So, wouldst thou keep thy spirit free from cloud,
A tranquil habit to thy latest day,
Follow the few, and not the vulgar crowd.
Yet mayest thou urge, "Brother, the very way
Thou showest us, wherefrom thy footsteps proud
(And never more than now) so oft did stray."

IN VITA. LXXVI.

Sennuccio, I would have thee know the shame
That 's dealt to me, and what a life is mine.
Even as of yore, I struggle, burn and pine.
Laura transports me, I am still the same.
All meekness here, all pride she there became,
Now harsh, now kind, now cruel, now benign;

Here honor clothed her, there a grace divine ;
Now gentle, now disdainful of my flame.
Here sweetly did she sing ; there sat awhile ;
There she turned back, she lingered in this spot.
Here with her splendid eyes my heart she clove.
She uttered there a word, and here did smile.
Here she changed color. Ah, in such fond
      thought,
Holds me by day and night, our master Love.

IN VITA. CV.

I saw on earth angelic graces beam,
  Celestial beauty in our world below,
Whose mere remembrance thrills with grief and
      woe ;
All I see now seems shadow, smoke and dream.
  I saw in those twin-lights the tear-drops gleam,
Those lights that made the sun with envy glow,
And from those lips such sighs and words did
     flow,
As made revolve the hills, stand still the stream.
Love, courage, wit, pity and pain in one,
  Wept in more dulcet and harmonious strain,
Than any other that the world has known.
  So rapt was heaven in the dear refrain,
That not a leaf upon the branch was blown,
  Such utter sweetness filled the aerial plain.

IN VITA. CIX.

THE God of Love and I in wonder stared,
(Ne'er having gazed on miracles ere now,)
Upon my lady's smiling lips and brow,
Who only with herself may be compared.
Neath the calm beauty of her forehead bared,
Those twin stars of my love did burn and flow,
No lesser lamps again the path might show
To the proud lover who by these had fared.
Oh miracle, when on the grass at rest,
Herself a flower, she would clasp and hold
A leafy branch against her snow-white breast.
What joy to see her, in the autumn cold,
Wander alone, with maiden thoughts possess'd,
Weaving a garland of dry, crispy gold!

IN MORTE. II. ON THE DEATH OF CARDINAL COLONNA AND LAURA.

THE noble Column, the green Laurel-tree
Are fall'n, that shaded once my weary mind.
Now I have lost what I shall never find,
From North to South, from Red to Indian Sea.
My double treasure Death has filched from me,
Which made me proud and happy midst my kind.
Nor may all empires of the world combined,
Nor Orient gems, nor gold restore the key.
But if this be according to Fate's will,
What may I do, but wander heavy-souled,
With ever downcast head, eyes weeping still?

O life of ours, so lovely to behold,
In one brief morn how easily dost thou spill
That which we toiled for years to gain and hold!

IN MORTE. XLIII.

YON nightingale who mourns so plaintively
Perchance his fledglings or his darling mate,
Fills sky and earth with sweetness, warbling late,
Prophetic notes of melting melody.
All night, he, as it were, companions me,
Reminding me of my so cruel fate,
Mourning no other grief save mine own state,
Who knew not Death reigned o'er divinity.
How easy 't is to dupe the soul secure!
Those two fair lamps, even than the sun more
          bright,
Who ever dreamed to see turn clay obscure?
But Fortune has ordained, I now am sure,
That I, midst lifelong tears, should learn aright,
Naught here can make us happy, or endure.

IN VITA. CANZONE XI.

O WATERS fresh and sweet and clear,
  Where bathed her lovely frame,
    Who seems the only lady unto me;
O gentle branch and dear,
  (Sighing I speak thy name,)
    Thou column for her shapely thighs, her
      supple knee;

O grass, O flowers, which she
   Swept with her gown that veiled
The angelic breast unseen;
   O sacred air serene,
Whence the divine-eyed Love my heart assailed,
   By all of ye be heard
This my supreme lament, my dying word.

    Oh, if it be my fate
    (As Heaven shall so decree)
That Love shall close for me my weeping eyes,
    Some courteous friend I supplicate
    Midst these to bury me,
Whilst my enfranchised spirit homeward flies;
    Less dreadful death shall rise,
If I may bear this hope
    To that mysterious goal.
For ne'er did weary soul
Find a more restful spot in all Earth's scope,
Nor in a grave more tranquil could win free
From outworn flesh and weary limbs to flee.

    Perchance the time shall be
    When to my place of rest,
With milder grace my wild fawn shall return
    Here where she looked on me
    Upon that day thrice blest:
Then she shall bend her radiant eyes that yearn
In search of me, and (piteous sight!) shall learn
That I, amidst the stones, am clay.

May love inspire her in such wise,
With gentlest breath of sighs,
That I, a stony corpse, shall hear her pray,
    And force the very skies,
That I may wipe the tears from her dear eyes.

From the fair boughs descended
    (Thrice precious memory!)
Upon her lap a shower of fragrant bloom
    Amidst that glory splendid,
    Humbly reposèd she,
Attired as with an aureole's golden gloom.
Some blossoms edged her skirt, and some
    Fell on her yellow curls,
Like burnished gold and pearls,
    Even so they looked to me upon that day.
Some on the ground, some on the river lay,
    Some lightly fluttering above,
Encircling her, seemed whispering: "Here reigns
    Love."

    How many times I cried,
    As holy fear o'ercame,
"Surely this creature sprang from Paradise,"
    Forgetting all beside
    Her goddess mien, her frame,
Her face, her words, her lovely smile, her eyes.
    All these did so devise
    To win me from the truth, alas!
    That I did say and sigh,

" How came I hither, when and why ? "
Deeming myself in heaven, not where I was.
    Henceforth this grassy spot
I love so much, peace elsewhere find I not.

    My Song, wert thou adorned to thy desire,
      Thou couldst go boldly forth
And wander from my lips o'er all the earth.

FRAGMENT. CANZONE XII. 5.

I NEVER see, after nocturnal rain,
The wandering stars move through the air serene,
And flame forth 'twixt the dew-fall and the rime,
But I behold her radiant eyes wherein
My weary spirit findeth rest from pain ;
As dimmed by her rich veil, I saw her the first
    time ;
The very heaven beamed with the light sublime
Of their celestial beauty ; dewy-wet
Still do they shine, and I am burning yet.
Now if the rising sun I see,
I feel the light that hath enamored me.
Or if he sets, I follow him, when he
Bears elsewhere his eternal light,
Leaving behind the shadowy waves of night.

FRAGMENT.   TRIONFO D' AMORE.

I KNOW how well Love shoots, how swift his
      flight,
How now by force and now by stealth he steals,
How he will threaten now, anon will smite,
And how unstable are his chariot wheels.
How doubtful are his hopes, how sure his pain,
And how his faithful promise he repeals.
How in one's marrow, in one's vital vein,
His smouldering fire quickens a hidden wound,
Where death is manifest, destruction plain.
In sum, how erring, fickle and unsound,
How timid and how bold are lovers' days,
Where with scant sweetness bitter draughts
      abound.
I know their songs, their sighs, their usual ways,
Their broken speech, their sudden silences.
Their passing laughter and their grief that stays,
I know how mixed with gall their honey is.

FRAGMENT.   TRIONFO DELLA MORTE.

Now since nor grief nor fear was longer there,
Each thought on her fair face was clear to see,
Composed into the calmness of despair —
Not like a flame extinguished violently,
But one consuming of its proper light.
Even so, in peace, serene of soul, passed she.
Even as a lamp, so lucid, softly-bright,

Whose sustenance doth fail by slow degrees,
Wearing unto the end, its wonted plight.
Not pale, but whiter than the snow one sees
Flaking a hillside through the windless air.
Like one o'erwearied, she reposed in peace
As 't were a sweet sleep filled each lovely eye,
The soul already having fled from there.
And this is what dull fools have named to die.
Upon her fair face death itself seemed fair.

TRANSLATIONS FROM ALFRED DE MUSSET.

THE MAY NIGHT.

MUSE.

GIVE me a kiss, my poet, take thy lyre;
The buds are bursting on the wild sweet-briar.
To-night the Spring is born — the breeze takes
    fire.
Expectant of the dawn behold the thrush,
Perched on the fresh branch of the first green
       bush;
Give me a kiss, my poet, take thy lyre.

POET.

How black it looks within the vale!
I thought a muffled form did sail
Above the tree-tops, through the air.
It seemed from yonder field to pass,
Its foot just grazed the tender grass;
A vision strange and fair it was.
It melts and is no longer there.

MUSE.

My poet, take thy lyre; upon the lawn
Night rocks the zephyr on her veiled, soft breast.

The rose, still virgin, holds herself withdrawn
From the winged, irised wasp with love pos-
       sessed.
Hark, all is hushed. Now of thy sweetheart
       dream ;
To-day the sunset, with a lingering beam,
Caressed the dusky-foliaged linden-grove.
All things shall bloom to-night ; great Nature
       thrills,
Her couch with perfume, passion, sighs, she fills,
Like to the nuptial bed of youthful love.

POET.

Why throbs my heart so fast, so low ?
What sets my seething blood aglow,
And fills my sense with vague affright ?
Who raps upon my chamber-door ?
My lamp's spent ray upon the floor,
Why does it dazzle me with light ?
Great God! my limbs sink under me !
Who enters ? who is calling ? none !
The clock strikes — I am all alone —
O solitude ! O poverty !

MUSE.

My poet, take thy lyre. Youth's living wine
Ferments to-night within the veins divine.
My breast is troubled, stifling with desire,
The panting breeze has set my lips afire ;
O listless child, behold me, I am fair !

Our first embrace dost thou so soon forget?
How pale thou wast, when my wing grazed thy
 hair.
Into mine arms thou fell'st, with eyelids wet!
Oh, in thy bitter grief, I solaced thee,
Dying of love, thy youthful strength outworn.
Now I shall die of hope — oh comfort me!
I need thy prayers to live until the morn.

POET.

Is it thy voice my spirit knows,
O darling Muse! And canst thou be
My own immortal one? my rose,
Sole pure and faithful heart where glows
A lingering spark of love for me?
Yes, it is thou, with tresses bright,
'T is thou, my sister and my bride.
I feel amidst the shadowy night,
From thy gold gown the rays of light
Within my heart's recesses glide.

MUSE.

My poet, take thy lyre.   'T is I, undying,
Who seeing thee to-night so sad and dumb,
Like to the mother - bird whose brood is cry-
 ing,
From utmost heaven to weep with thee have
 come.
My friend, thou sufferest; a secret woe
Gnaws at thy life, thou sighest in the night.

Love visits thee, such love as mortals know,
Shadow of gladness, semblance of delight.
Rise, sing to God the thoughts that fill thy
    brain,
Thy buried pleasures and thy long-past pain.
Come, with a kiss, where unknown regions
    gleam,
Awake the mingling echoes of thy days,
Sing of thy folly, glory, joy and praise,
Be all an unpremeditated dream!
Let us invent a realm where one forgets,
Come, we are all alone, the world is ours.
Green Scotland tawny Italy offsets;
Lo, Greece my mother, with her honeyed
    flowers,
Argos and Pteleon with its shrines and groves,
Celestial Messa populous with doves;
And Pelion with his shaggy, changing brow,
Blue Titaresus, and the gulf of steel,
Whose waves that glass the floating swan, reveal
Snowy Camyre to Oloossone's snow.
Tell me what golden dreams shall charm our
    sleep,
Whence shall be drawn the tears that we shall
    weep?
This morning when thy lids were touched with
    light,
What pensive seraph, bending kindly near,
Dropped lilacs from his airy robe of white,
And whispered dreams of love within thine ear?

Say, shall we sing of sadness, joy or hope?
Or bathe in blood the serried, steel-clad ranks?
See lovers mount the ladder's silken rope?
Or fleck the wind with coursers' foaming flanks?
Or shall we tell whose hand the lamps above,
In the celestial mansions, year by year,
Kindles with sacred oil of life and love?
With Tarquin shall we cry, " Come, night is
   here ! "
Or shall we dive for pearls beneath the seas,
Or find the wild goats by the alpine trees?
Bid melancholy gaze upon the skies?
Follow the huntsman on the upland lawns?
The roe uplifts her tearful, suppliant eyes,
Her heath awaits her, and her suckling fawns;
He stoops, he slaughters her, he flings her heart
Still warm amidst his panting hounds apart.
Or shall we paint a maid with vermeil cheek,
Who, with her page behind, to vespers fares,
Beside her mother, dreamy-eyed and meek,
And on her half-oped lips forgets her prayers,
Trembles midst echoing columns, hearkening
To hear her bold knight's clanging spurs out-
   ring.
Or shall we bid the heroes of old France
Scale full equipped the battlemented wall,
And so revive the simple-strained romance
Their fame inspired our troubadours withal?
Or shall we clothe soft elegies in white?
Or bid the man of Waterloo recite

His story, and the crop mown by his art,
Or ere the herald of eternal night
On his green mound with fatal wing did smite
And cross his hands above his iron heart?
Or shall we gibbet on some satire here
The name thrice - bought of some pale pam-
   phleteer,
Who, hunger-goaded, from his haunts obscure,
Dared, quivering with impotence and spite,
Insult the hope on Genius' brow of light,
And gnaw the wreath his breath had made im-
   pure?
The lyre! the lyre! I can be still no more.
Upon the breath of spring my pinions fly.
The air supports me — from the earth I soar,
Thou weepest — God has heard — the hour is
   nigh!

POET.

Dear sister, if thou ask but this,
From friendly lips a gentle kiss,
Or one soft tear from kindly eyes,
These will I gladly give to thee.
Our love remember tenderly,
If thou remountest to the skies.
No longer I of hope shall sing,
Of fame or joy, of love or art,
Alas, not even of suffering,
My lips are locked — I lean and cling,
To hear the whisper of my heart.

MUSE.

What! am I like the autumn breeze for you,
Which feeds on tears even to the very grave,
For whom all grief is but a drop of dew?
O poet, but one kiss — 't was I who gave.
The weed I fain would root from out this sod
Is thine own sloth — thy grief belongs to God.
Whatever sorrow thy young heart have found,
Open it well, this ever-sacred wound
Dealt by dark angels — give thy soul relief.
Naught makes us nobler than a noble grief.
Yet deem not, poet, though this pain have come,
That therefore, here below, thou mayst be
      dumb.
Best are the songs most desperate in their
      woe —
Immortal ones, which are pure sobs I know.
When the wave-weary pelican once more,
Midst evening-vapors, gains his nest of reeds,
His famished brood run forward on the shore
To see where high above the surge he speeds.
As though even now their prey they could de-
      stroy,
They hasten to their sire with screams of joy,
On swollen necks wagging their beaks, they
      cry;
He slowly wins at last a lofty rock,
Shelters beneath his drooping wing his flock,
And, a sad fisher, gazes on the sky.

Adown his open breast the blood flows there ;
Vainly he searched the ocean's deepest part,
The sea was empty and the shore was bare,
And for all nourishment he brings his heart.
Sad, silent, on the stone, he gives his brood
His father-entrails and his father-blood,
Lulls with his love sublime his cruel pain,
And, watching on his breast the ruddy stain,
Swoons at the fatal banquet from excess
Of horror and voluptuous tenderness.
Sudden amidst the sacrifice divine,
Outworn with such protracted suffering,
He fears his flock may let him live and pine ;
Then up he starts, expands his mighty wing,
Beating his heart, and with a savage cry
Bids a farewell of such funereal tone
That the scared seabirds from their rock-nests
      fly,
And the late traveller on the beach alone
Commends his soul to God — for death floats by.
Even such, O poet, is the poet's fate.
His life sustains the creatures of a day.
The banquets served upon his feasts of state
Are like the pelican's — sublime as they.
And when he tells the world of hopes betrayed,
Forgetfulness and grief, of love and hate,
His music does not make the heart dilate,
His eloquence is as an unsheathed blade,
Tracing a glittering circle in mid-air,
While blood drips from the edges keen and bare.

POET.

O Muse, insatiate soul, demand
   No more than lies in human power.
Man writes no word upon the sand
   Even at the furious whirlwind's hour.
There was a time when joyous youth
   Forever fluttered at my mouth,
A merry, singing bird, just freed.
   Strange martyrdom has since been mine,
Should I revive its slightest sign,
   At the first note, my lyre and thine
Would snap asunder like a reed.

THE OCTOBER NIGHT.

POET.

My haunting grief has vanished like a dream,
   Its floating fading memory seems one
With those frail mists born of the dawn's first
      beam,
   Dissolving as the dew melts in the sun.

MUSE.

   What ailed thee then, O poet mine ;
   What secret misery was thine,
   Which set a bar 'twixt thee and me ?
   Alas, I suffer from it still ;

What was this grief, this unknown ill,
Which I have wept so bitterly ?

POET.

'T was but a common grief, well known of men.
   But, look you, when our heavy heart is sore,
Fond wretches that we are ! we fancy then
   That sorrow never has been felt before.

MUSE.

There cannot be a common grief,
   Save that of common souls ; my friend,
Speak out, and give thy heart relief,
   Of this grim secret make an end.
Confide in me, and have no fear.
The God of silence, pale, austere,
   Is younger brother unto death.
Even as we mourn we 're comforted,
And oft a single word is said
Which from remorse delivereth.

POET.

If I were bound this day to tell my woe,
   I know not by what name to call my pain,
Love, folly, pride, experience — neither know
   If one in all the world might thereby gain.
Yet ne'ertheless I 'll voice the tale to thee,
Alone here by the hearth.   But do thou take
This lyre — come nearer — so ; my memory
Shall gently with the harmonies awake.

MUSE.

But first, or ere thy grief thou say,
   My poet, art thou healed thereof ?
Bethink thee, thou must speak to-day,
   As free from hatred as from love.
For man has given the holy name
     Of consolation unto me.
Make me no partner of thy shame,
In passions that have ruined thee.

POET.

Of my old wounds I am so sound and whole,
   Almost I doubt they were, nor find their trace ;
And in the passes where I risked my soul,
   In mine own stead I see a stranger's face.
Muse, have no fear, we both may yield awhile
   To this first inspiration of regret.
Oh, it is good to weep, 't is good to smile,
   Remembering sorrows we might else forget.

MUSE.

As the watchful mother stoops
   O'er her infant's cradled rest,
So my trembling spirit droops
   O'er this long-closed, silent breast.
Speak ! I touch the lyre's sweet strings,
   Feebly, plaintively it sings,
With thy voice set free at last.
   While athwart a radiant beam,

Like a light, enchanted dream,
  Float the shadows of the past.

POET.

My days of work! sole days whereon I lived!
  O thrice-belovèd solitude!
Now God be praised, once more I have arrived
  In this old study bare and rude.
These oft-deserted walls, this shabby den,
  My faithful lamp, my dusty chair,
My palace, my small world I greet again,
  My Muse, immortal, young and fair.
Thank God! we twain may sing here side by
    side,
  I will reveal to thee my thought.
Thou shalt know all, to thee I will confide
  The evil by a woman wrought.
A woman, yes! (mayhap, poor friends, ye guess,
  Or ever I have said the word!)
To such a one my soul was bound, no less
  Than is the vassal to his lord.
Detested yoke! within me to destroy
  The vigor and the bloom of youth!
Yet only through my love I caught, in sooth,
  A fleeting glimpse of joy.
When by the brook, beneath the evening-star,
  On silver sands we twain would stray,
The white wraith of the aspen tree afar
  Pointed for us the dusky way.
Once more within the moonlight do I see

That fair form sink upon my breast;
No more of that!   Alas, I never guessed
    Whither my fate was leading me.
The angry gods some victim craved, I fear,
    At that ill-omened time,
Since they have punished me as for a crime,
    For trying to be happy here!

MUSE.

A vision of remembered joy
    Reveals itself to thee once more;
Why fearest thou to live it o'er,
    Retracing it without annoy?
Wouldst thou confide the truth to me,
    And yet those golden days disprove?
If fate has been unkind to thee,
    Do thou no less, my friend, than she,
And smile upon thine early love.

POET.

Rather I dare to smile upon my woe.
    Muse, I have said it, I would fain review
My crosses, visions, frenzy, — calmly show
    The hour, place, circumstance, in order due.
'T was an autumnal evening, I recall,
    Chill, gloomy; this one brings it back again.
The murmuring wind's monotonous rise and fall
    Lulled sombre care within my weary brain.
I waited at the casement for my love,
    And listening in the darkness black as death,

Such melancholy did my spirit move
   That all at once I doubted of her faith.
The street wherein I dwelt was lonely, poor,
   Lantern in hand, at times, a shade passed by,
When the gale whistled through the half-oped
     door.
   One seemed to hear afar a human sigh.
I know not to what omen, sooth to say,
   My superstitious spirit fell a prey.
Vainly I summoned courage — coward-like
   I shuddered when the clock began to strike.
She did not come! Alone, with downcast head,
   I stared at street and walls like one possessed.
How may I tell the insensate passion bred
   By that inconstant woman in my breast!
I loved but her in all the world. One day
   Apart from her seemed worse than death to me.
Yet I remember how I did essay
   That cruel night to snap my chain, go free.
I named her traitress, serpent, o'er and o'er,
   Recalled the anguish suffered for her sake,
Alas! her fatal beauty rose once more,
   What grief, what torture in my heart to wake!
At last morn broke; with waiting vain outworn,
   I fell asleep against the casement there.
I oped my lids upon the day new born,
   My dazzled glance swam in the radiant air.
Then on the outer staircase, suddenly,
   I heard soft steps ascend the narrow flight.
Save me, Great God! I see her — it is she!

Whence com'st thou? speak, where hast thou
    been this night?
What dost thou seek? who brings thee here thus
    late?
Where has this lovely form reclined till day,
While I alone must watch and weep and wait?
    Where, and on whom hast thou been smiling,
      say!
Out, insolent traitress! canst thou come accurst,
    And offer to my kiss thy lips' ripe charms?
What cravest thou? By what unhallowed thirst
    Darest thou allure me to thy jaded arms?
Avaunt, begone! ghost of my mistress dead,
    Back to thy grave! avoid the morning's beam!
Be my lost youth no more rememberèd!
    And when I think of thee, I'll know it was a
      dream!

MUSE.

Be calm! I beg thee, I implore!
    I shudder, hearing of thy pain.
O dearest friend, thy wound once more
    Is opening to bleed again.
Is it so very deep, alas!
How slowly do the traces pass
Of this world's troubles! Thou, my son,
Forget her! let thy memory shun
Even to this woman's very name,
My pitying lips refuse to frame.

POET.

Shame upon her, who first
   Treason and falsehood taught!
With grief and wrath accurst,
   Who set my brain distraught.
Shame, woman baleful-eyed,
   Whose fatal love entombed
In shadows of thy pride
   My April ere it bloomed.
It was thy voice, thy smile,
   Thy poisoned glances bright,
Which taught me to revile
   The semblance of delight.
Thy grace of girlish years
   Murdered my peace, my sleep.
If I lose faith in tears,
   'T is that I saw thee weep.
I yielded to thy power
   A child's simplicity.
As to the dawn the flower,
   So oped my heart to thee.
Doubtless this helpless heart
   Was thine without defence.
Were 't not the better part
   To spare its innocence?
Shame! thou who didst beget
   My earliest, youngest woe.
The tears are streaming yet
   Which first thou madest flow.

Quenchless this source is found
    Which thou hast first unsealed.
It issues from a wound
    That never may be healed.
But in the bitter wave
    I shall be clean restored,
And from my soul shall lave
    Thy memory abhorred!

MUSE.

Poet, enough! Though but one single day
    Lasted thy dream of her who faithless proved,
That day insult not; whatsoe'er thou say,
    Respect thy love, if thou would be beloved.
If human weakness find the task too great
    Of pardoning the wrongs by others done,
At least the torture spare thyself of hate,
    In place of pardon seek oblivion.
The dead lie peaceful in the earth asleep,
    So our extinguished passions too, should rest.
Dust are those relics also; let us keep
    Our hands from violence to their ashes blest.
Why, in this story of keen pain, my friend,
    Wilt thou refuse naught but a dream to see?
Does Nature causeless act, to no wise end?
    Think'st thou a heedless God afflicted thee?
Mayhap the blow thou weepest was to save.
    Child, it has oped thy heart to seek relief;
Sorrow is lord to man, and man a slave,
    None knows himself till he has walked with
        grief, —

A cruel law, but none the less supreme,
   Old as the world, yea, old as destiny.
Sorrow baptizes us, a fatal scheme;
   All things at this sad price we still must buy.
The harvest needs the dew to make it ripe,
   And man to live, to feel, has need of tears.
Joy chooses a bruised plant to be her type,
   That, drenched with rain, still many a blossom
      bears.
Didst thou not say this folly long had slept?
   Art thou not happy, young, a welcome guest?
And those light pleasures that give life its zest,
   How wouldst thou value if thou hadst not wept?
When, lying in the sunlight on the grass,
   Freely thou drink'st with some old friend —
      confess,
Wouldst thou so cordially uplift thy glass,
   Hadst thou not weighed the worth of cheer-
      fulness?
Would flowers be so dear unto thy heart,
   The verse of Petrarch, warblings of the bird,
Shakespeare and Nature, Angelo and Art,
   But that thine ancient sobs therein thou heard?
Couldst thou conceive the ineffable peace of
      heaven,
   Night's silence, murmurs of the wave that
      flows,
If sleeplessness and fever had not driven
   Thy thought to yearn for infinite repose?
By a fair woman's love art thou not blest?

When thou dost hold and clasp her hand in
    thine,
Does not the thought of woes that once possessed,
    Make all the sweeter now her smile divine?
Wander ye not together, thou and she,
    Midst blooming woods, on sands like silver
      bright?
Does not the white wraith of the aspen-tree
    In that green palace, mark the path at night?
And seest thou not, within the moon's pale ray,
    Her lovely form sink on thy breast again?
If thou shouldst meet with Fortune on thy way,
    Wouldst thou not follow singing, in her train?
What hast thou to regret? Immortal Hope
    Is shaped anew in thee by Sorrow's hand.
Why hate experience that enlarged thy scope?
    Why curse the pain that made thy soul ex-
      pand?
Oh pity her! so false, so fair to see,
    Who from thine eyes such bitter tears did
      press,
She was a woman. God revealed to thee,
    Through her, the secret of all happiness.
Her task was hard; she loved thee, it may be,
    Yet must she break thy heart, so fate decreed.
She knew the world, she taught it unto thee,
    Another reaps the fruit of her misdeed.
Pity her! dreamlike did her love disperse,
    She saw thy wound — nor could thy pain re-
      move.

All was not falsehood in those tears of hers —
    Pity her, though it were, — for thou canst
        love!

POET.

True!   Hate is blasphemy.
    With horror's thrill, I start,
This sleeping snake to see,
    Uncoil within my heart.
Oh Goddess, hear my cries,
    My vow to thee is given,
By my beloved's blue eyes,
    And by the azure heaven,
By yonder spark of flame,
    Yon trembling pearl, the star
That beareth Venus' name,
    And glistens from afar,
By Nature's glorious scheme,
    The infinite grace of God,
The planet's tranquil beam
    That cheers the traveler's road,
The grass, the water-course,
    Woods, fields with dew impearled,
The quenchless vital force,
    The sap of all the world, —
I banish from my heart
    This reckless passion's ghost,
Mysterious shade, depart!
    In the dark past be lost!
And thou whom once I met

As friend, while thou didst live,
　The hour when I forget,
　　I likewise should forgive.
Let me forgive !　I break
　The long-uniting spell.
With a last tear, oh take,
　Take thou, a last farewell.
Now, gold-haired, pensive Muse,
　On to our pleasures !　Sing —
Some joyous carol choose,
　As in the dear old Spring.
Mark, how the dew-drenched lawn
　Scents the auroral hour.
Waken my love with dawn,
　And pluck her garden's flower.
Immortal nature, see !
　Casts slumber's veil away.
New born with her are we
　In morning's earliest ray.

NOTES TO "EPISTLE" OF JOSHUA IBN VIVES OF ALLORQUI.

◆

THE life and character of Paulus de Santa Maria are thus described by Dr. Graetz : —

Among the Jews baptized in 1391, no other wrought so much harm to his race as the Rabbi Solomon Levi of Burgos, known to Christians as Paulus Burgensis, or de Santa Maria (born about 1351–52, died 1435) who rose to very high ecclesiastical and political rank. . . . He had no philosophical culture ; on the contrary, as a Jew, he had been extremely devout, observing scrupulously all the rites, and regarded as a pillar of Judaism in his own circle. . . . Possessed by ambition and vanity, the synagogue where he had passed a short time in giving and receiving instruction, appeared to him too narrow and restricted a sphere. He longed for a bustling activity, aimed at a position at court, in whatever capacity, began to live on a grand scale, maintained a sumptuous equipage, a spirited team, and a numerous retinue of servants. As his affairs brought him into daily contact with Christians and entangled him in religious discussions, he studied ecclesiastical literature in order to display his erudition. The bloody massacre of 1391 robbed him of all hope of reaching eminence as a Jew, in his fortieth year, and he abruptly resolved to be baptized. The lofty degree of dignity which he afterwards at-

tained in Church and State, may even then have
floated alluringly before his mind. In order to
profit by his apostasy, the convert Paulus de Santa
Maria gave out that he had voluntarily embraced
Christianity, the theological writings of the Scholiast
Thomas of Aquinas having taken hold of his inmost
convictions. The Jews, however, mistrusted his
credulity, and knowing him well, they ascribed this
step to his ambition and his thirst for fame. His
family, consisting of a wife and son, renounced him
when he changed his faith. . . . He studied theology
in the University of Paris, and then visited the papal
court of Avignon, where Cardinal Pedro de Juna had
been elected papal antagonist to Benedict XIII. of
Rome. The church feud and the schism between
the two Popes offered the most favorable opportu-
nity for intrigues and claims. Paulus, by his clever-
ness, his zeal, and his eloquence, won the favor of the
Pope, who discerned in him a useful tool. Thus he
became successively Archdeacon of Trevinjo, Canon
of Seville, Bishop of Cartagena, Chancellor of Cas-
tile, and Privy Councillor to King Henry III. of
Spain. With tongue and pen he attacked Judaism,
and Jewish literature provided him with the neces-
sary weapons. Intelligent Jews rightly divined in
this convert to Christianity their bitterest enemy,
and entered into a contest with him. . . .

The campaign against the malignity of Paul de
Santa Maria was opened by a young man who had
formerly sat at his feet, Joshua ben Joseph Ibn
Vives, from the town of Lorca or Allorqui, a physi-
cian and Arabic scholar. In an epistle written in a
tone of humility as from a docile pupil to a revered
master, he deals his apostate teacher heavy blows,

and under the show of doubt he shatters the founda-
tions of Christianity. He begins by saying that the
apostasy of his beloved teacher to whom his loyal
spirit had formerly clung, has amazed him beyond
measure and aroused in him many serious reflections.
He can only conceive four possible motives for such
a surprising step. Either Paulus has been actuated
by ambition, love of wealth, pomp, and the satisfac-
tion of the senses, or else by doubt of the truth of
Judaism upon philosophic grounds, and has re-
nounced therefore the religion which afforded him so
little freedom and security ; or else he has foreseen
through the latest cruel persecutions of the Jews in
Spain, the total extinction of the race ; or, finally, he
may have become convinced of the truth of Christi-
anity. The writer enters therefore into an examina-
tion based upon his acquaintance with the character of
his former master, as to which of these four motives
is most likely to have occasioned the act. He cannot
believe that ambition and covetousness prompted it,
" For I remember when you used to be surrounded
by wealth and attendants, you sighed regretfully
for your previous humble station, for your retired
life and communion with wisdom, and regarded your
actual brilliant position as an unsatisfactory sham
happiness. Neither can Allorqui admit that Paulus
had been disturbed by philosophic scepticism, for to
the day of his baptism he had observed all the Jew-
ish customs and had only accepted that little kernel
of philosophy which accords with faith, always re-
jecting the pernicious outward shell. He must also
discard the theory that the sanguinary persecution of
the Jews could have made Paulus despair of the pos-
sible continuation of the Jewish race, for only a small

portion of the Jews dwelt among Christians, while the majority lived in Asia and enjoyed a certain independence. There remains only the conclusion that Paulus has tested the new dogmas and found them sufficient. . . . Allorqui therefore begs him to communicate his convictions and vanquish his pupil's doubts concerning Christianity. Instead of the general spread of divine doctrine and everlasting peace which the prophets had associated with the advent of the Messiah, only dissension and war reigned on earth. Indeed, after Jesus' appearance, frightful wars had but increased. . . . And even if Allorqui conceded the Messiahship of Jesus, the Immaculate Conception, the Resurrection, and all incomprehensible miracles, he could not reconcile himself to the idea of God becoming a man. Every enlightened conception of the Deity was at variance with it."

[Page 77 et seq. Volume 8, Second half, Graetz' History of the Jews.]

MARRANO. — See Verse xix., Line 7th of "Epistle."

The enforced recipients of baptism who remained in Spain formed a peculiar class, outwardly Christians, inwardly Jews. They might have been called Jewish-Christians. They were looked upon with suspicion by the Christian population, and shunned with a still more intense hatred by the loyal Jews who gave them the name of Marranos, the accursed. [Page 73.]

> "Master, if thou to thy prides' goal should come,
> Where wouldst thou throne — at Avignon or Rome?"
>
> Verse xxviii. 7, 8.

This sentence occurs in another Epistle to Paulus by Profiat Duran.

Verses 29 and 30 are paraphrases from an epistle to Paulus by Chasdai Crescas.

"These are burning questions, from which the fire of the stake may be kindled. Christianity gives itself out as a new revelation in a certain sense completing and improving Judaism. But the revelation has so little efficacy, that in the prolonged schism in the Church, a new divine message is already needed to scatter the dangerous errors. Two Popes and their partisans fulminate against each other bulls of excommunication and condemn each other to profoundest hell. Where is the truth and certainty of revelation?" [Graetz' History of the Jews.]

DOVER·THRIFT·EDITIONS

POETRY

DOVER · THRIFT · EDITIONS

POETRY

GREAT POEMS BY AMERICAN WOMEN: An Anthology, Edited by Susan L. Rattiner. (0-486-40164-2)

FAVORITE POEMS, Henry Wadsworth Longfellow. (0-486-27273-7)

BHAGAVADGITA, Translated by Sir Edwin Arnold. (0-486-27782-8)

ESSAY ON MAN AND OTHER POEMS, Alexander Pope. (0-486-28053-5)

GREAT LOVE POEMS, Edited by Shane Weller. (0-486-27284-2)

DOVER BEACH AND OTHER POEMS, Matthew Arnold. (0-486-28037-3)

THE SHOOTING OF DAN MCGREW AND OTHER POEMS, Robert Service. (0-486-27556-6)

THE BALLAD OF READING GAOL AND OTHER POEMS, Oscar Wilde. (0-486-27072-6)

SELECTED POEMS OF RUMI, Jalalu'l-Din Rumi. (0-486-41583-X)

SELECTED POEMS OF GERARD MANLEY HOPKINS, Gerard Manley Hopkins. Edited and with an Introduction by Bob Blaisdell. (0-486-47867-X)

RENASCENCE AND OTHER POEMS, Edna St. Vincent Millay. (0-486-26873-X)

THE RUBÁIYÁT OF OMAR KHAYYÁM: First and Fifth Editions, Edward FitzGerald. (0-486-26467-X)

TO MY HUSBAND AND OTHER POEMS, Anne Bradstreet. (0-486-41408-6)

LITTLE ORPHANT ANNIE AND OTHER POEMS, James Whitcomb Riley. (0-486-28260-0)

IMAGIST POETRY: AN ANTHOLOGY, Edited by Bob Blaisdell. (0-486-40875-2)

FIRST FIG AND OTHER POEMS, Edna St. Vincent Millay. (0-486-41104-4)

GREAT SHORT POEMS FROM ANTIQUITY TO THE TWENTIETH CENTURY, Edited by Dorothy Belle Pollack. (0-486-47876-9)

THE FLOWERS OF EVIL & PARIS SPLEEN: Selected Poems, Charles Baudelaire. Translated by Wallace Fowlie. (0-486-47545-X)

CIVIL WAR SHORT STORIES AND POEMS, Edited by Bob Blaisdell. (0-486-48226-X)

EARLY POEMS, Edna St. Vincent Millay. (0-486-43672-1)

JABBERWOCKY AND OTHER POEMS, Lewis Carroll. (0-486-41582-1)

THE METAMORPHOSES: Selected Stories in Verse, Ovid. (0-486-42758-7)

IDYLLS OF THE KING, Alfred, Lord Tennyson. Edited by W. J. Rolfe. (0-486-43795-7)

A BOY'S WILL AND NORTH OF BOSTON, Robert Frost. (0-486-26866-7)

100 FAVORITE ENGLISH AND IRISH POEMS, Edited by Clarence C. Strowbridge. (0-486-44429-5)

DOVER·THRIFT·EDITIONS

FICTION

FLATLAND: A ROMANCE OF MANY DIMENSIONS, Edwin A. Abbott.
(0-486-27263-X)

PRIDE AND PREJUDICE, Jane Austen. (0-486-28473-5)

CIVIL WAR SHORT STORIES AND POEMS, Edited by Bob Blaisdell.
(0-486-48226-X)

THE DECAMERON: Selected Tales, Giovanni Boccaccio. Edited by Bob Blaisdell. (0-486-41113-3)

JANE EYRE, Charlotte Brontë. (0-486-42449-9)

WUTHERING HEIGHTS, Emily Brontë. (0-486-29256-8)

THE THIRTY-NINE STEPS, John Buchan. (0-486-28201-5)

ALICE'S ADVENTURES IN WONDERLAND, Lewis Carroll. (0-486-27543-4)

MY ÁNTONIA, Willa Cather. (0-486-28240-6)

THE AWAKENING, Kate Chopin. (0-486-27786-0)

HEART OF DARKNESS, Joseph Conrad. (0-486-26464-5)

LORD JIM, Joseph Conrad. (0-486-40650-4)

THE RED BADGE OF COURAGE, Stephen Crane. (0-486-26465-3)

THE WORLD'S GREATEST SHORT STORIES, Edited by James Daley.
(0-486-44716-2)

A CHRISTMAS CAROL, Charles Dickens. (0-486-26865-9)

GREAT EXPECTATIONS, Charles Dickens. (0-486-41586-4)

A TALE OF TWO CITIES, Charles Dickens. (0-486-40651-2)

CRIME AND PUNISHMENT, Fyodor Dostoyevsky. Translated by Constance Garnett. (0-486-41587-2)

THE ADVENTURES OF SHERLOCK HOLMES, Sir Arthur Conan Doyle.
(0-486-47491-7)

THE HOUND OF THE BASKERVILLES, Sir Arthur Conan Doyle. (0-486-28214-7)

BLAKE: PROPHET AGAINST EMPIRE, David V. Erdman. (0-486-26719-9)

WHERE ANGELS FEAR TO TREAD, E. M. Forster. (0-486-27791-7)

BEOWULF, Translated by R. K. Gordon. (0-486-27264-8)

THE RETURN OF THE NATIVE, Thomas Hardy. (0-486-43165-7)

THE SCARLET LETTER, Nathaniel Hawthorne. (0-486-28048-9)

SIDDHARTHA, Hermann Hesse. (0-486-40653-9)

THE ODYSSEY, Homer. (0-486-40654-7)

THE TURN OF THE SCREW, Henry James. (0-486-26684-2)

DUBLINERS, James Joyce. (0-486-26870-5)

DOVER · THRIFT · EDITIONS

NONFICTION

POETICS, Aristotle. (0-486-29577-X)

MEDITATIONS, Marcus Aurelius. (0-486-29823-X)

THE WAY OF PERFECTION, St. Teresa of Avila. Edited and Translated by
E. Allison Peers. (0-486-48451-3)

THE DEVIL'S DICTIONARY, Ambrose Bierce. (0-486-27542-6)

GREAT SPEECHES OF THE 20TH CENTURY, Edited by Bob Blaisdell.
(0-486-47467-4)

THE COMMUNIST MANIFESTO AND OTHER REVOLUTIONARY WRITINGS:
Marx, Marat, Paine, Mao Tse-Tung, Gandhi and Others, Edited by Bob Blaisdell.
(0-486-42465-0)

INFAMOUS SPEECHES: From Robespierre to Osama bin Laden, Edited by Bob
Blaisdell. (0-486-47849-1)

GREAT ENGLISH ESSAYS: From Bacon to Chesterton, Edited by Bob Blaisdell.
(0-486-44082-6)

GREEK AND ROMAN ORATORY, Edited by Bob Blaisdell. (0-486-49622-8)

THE UNITED STATES CONSTITUTION: The Full Text with Supplementary
Materials, Edited and with supplementary materials by Bob Blaisdell.
(0-486-47166-7)

GREAT SPEECHES BY NATIVE AMERICANS, Edited by Bob Blaisdell.
(0-486-41122-2)

GREAT SPEECHES BY AFRICAN AMERICANS: Frederick Douglass, Sojourner
Truth, Dr. Martin Luther King, Jr., Barack Obama, and Others, Edited by
James Daley. (0-486-44761-8)

GREAT SPEECHES BY AMERICAN WOMEN, Edited by James Daley.
(0-486-46141-6)

HISTORY'S GREATEST SPEECHES, Edited by James Daley. (0-486-49739-9)

GREAT INAUGURAL ADDRESSES, Edited by James Daley. (0-486-44577-1)

GREAT SPEECHES ON GAY RIGHTS, Edited by James Daley. (0-486-47512-3)

ON THE ORIGIN OF SPECIES: By Means of Natural Selection, Charles Darwin.
(0-486-45006-6)

NARRATIVE OF THE LIFE OF FREDERICK DOUGLASS, Frederick Douglass.
(0-486-28499-9)

THE SOULS OF BLACK FOLK, W. E. B. Du Bois. (0-486-28041-1)

NATURE AND OTHER ESSAYS, Ralph Waldo Emerson. (0-486-46947-6)

SELF-RELIANCE AND OTHER ESSAYS, Ralph Waldo Emerson. (0-486-27790-9)

THE LIFE OF OLAUDAH EQUIANO, Olaudah Equiano. (0-486-40661-X)

WIT AND WISDOM FROM POOR RICHARD'S ALMANACK, Benjamin Franklin.
(0-486-40891-4)

THE AUTOBIOGRAPHY OF BENJAMIN FRANKLIN, Benjamin Franklin.
(0-486-29073-5)